Michael Price

Microsoft
365

in
easy steps

also covers Office 2019

In easy steps is an imprint of In Easy Steps Limited
16 Hamilton Terrace · Holly Walk · Leamington Spa
Warwickshire · United Kingdom · CV32 4LY
www.ineasysteps.com

Notice of Liability
Every effort has been made to ensure that this book contains accurate
and current information. However, In Easy Steps Limited and the
author shall not be liable for any loss or damage suffered by readers
as a result of any information contained herein.

Trademarks
Microsoft®, Microsoft 365®, Office 365® and Windows® are
registered trademarks of Microsoft Corporation. All other trademarks
are acknowledged as belonging to their respective companies.

In Easy Steps Limited supports The Forest Stewardship Council (FSC),
the leading international forest certification organization. All our titles
that are printed on Greenpeace approved FSC certified paper carry the
FSC logo.

MIX
Paper from
responsible sources
FSC www.fsc.org FSC® C020837

Printed and bound in the United Kingdom

ISBN 978-1-84078-935-5

Contents

1   **Introducing Microsoft 365**   **7**

Microsoft Office	8
Ribbon Technology	9
What's Needed	10
Installing Microsoft Office	11
Start an Application	12
Application Start	14
The Application Window	15
Your OneDrive	16
Live Preview	18
Working with the Ribbon	19
Quick Access Toolbar	20
Office Document Types	21
File Extensions	22
Compatibility Mode	23
Convert to the Latest Office Format	24

2   **Create Word Documents**   **25**

Create a Word Document	26
Enter Text	27
Select and Copy Text	28
Save the Document	30
Correct Proofing Errors	31
Change Proofing Settings	32
Apply Styles	33
Outline View	34
Insert a Picture	36
Page Layout	38
Display in Columns	39
Word Count	40
Create a Table	41
Convert Text to Table	42
Paste Special	43
Print Document	44

3   **Complex Documents**   **45**

Start a Booklet	46
Choose Page Arrangement	47
Create the Structure	48
Import Text	50
Insert Illustrations	52
Add Captions	53
Table of Contents	54
Table of Figures	56

Insert Preface   58
Update Table of Contents   59
Decorate the Page   60
Templates   62
Publisher   64
Create a Publication   65
Print the Publication   66

4   Calculations   67

Start Excel   68
Enter Data   70
Quick Fill   72
Sums and Differences   74
Formatting   76
Rounding Up   78
Find a Function   80
Goal Seeking   82
Templates   84

5   Manage Data   85

Import Data   86
Explore the Data   88
Sort   89
Filters   91
Number Filters   92
Select Specific Data   93
Create a Chart   94
Import a List   96
Create a Table   97
Add Totals to Table   98
Computed Column   100
Table Lookup   102
Manage Data using Access   104
Add Records   106

6   Presentations   107

Start a Presentation   108
Expand the Slide   110
Insert a Picture   111
Apply a Theme   112
Animations   114
Run the Show   115
Other Views   116
Presenter View   118
Choose a Template   120
Use the Template   122
Print the Slide Show   123
Rehearse Timings   124
Save As Options   125
Package for CD   126

7 Office Extras 127

Office Tools	128
Database Compare	129
Office Language Preferences	130
Spreadsheet Compare	132
Microsoft Store Tools	134
Office Lens	136
Third Party Office Tools	138
Windows 10 Tools	140
OneNote	142
OneNote 2016	144

8 Email 145

Starting Outlook	146
Your First Messages	148
Turn Off Reading Pane	149
Request a Newsletter	150
Receive a Message	152
Save All Attachments	154
Print the Message	155
Reply to the Message	156
Add Address to Contacts	157
Spam and Phishing	158
Create a Message	160
Insert a Signature	161
Message Tags	162
RSS Feeds	163

9 Time Management 165

Outlook Calendar	166
Schedule an Appointment	167
Change Appointment Details	168
Recurring Appointments	169
Create a Meeting	170
Respond to an Invitation	172
Add Holidays	174
Report Free/Busy Time	176
Schedule a Meeting	177
Creating Tasks	178
Assigning Tasks	180
Accepting Task Requests	181
Confirming the Assignment	182
Outlook Notes	184
Journal	186

10   Manage Files and Fonts   187

Device Setup	188
Library Location	190
Finding Files	191
Recent Documents	193
Change File Type	194
XML File Formats	195
Save As PDF or XPS	196
Fonts in Office	198
Create and Run ListAllFonts	200
Document Recovery	202

11   Up-to-Date and Secure   203

Office Updates	204
Apply Updates	206
Change Settings	207
Office Help	208
Explore Help Topics	209
Developer Tab	210
Remove Personal Information	212
Protect Your Documents	214
Restrict Permission	216
Trust Center	218

12   More Office Apps   219

Microsoft Teams	220
Microsoft Forms	221
Project	222
Visio	224
Microsoft Sway	226
Office Online	228
Office for iOS	230
More Office Mobile	232

Index   233

1 Introducing Microsoft 365

This chapter discusses the latest version of Microsoft Office, with its ribbon-style user interface. It identifies the range of editions, and outlines the requirements for installation. Also covered are: the process of starting applications; features used by all Office applications such as Preview and Save; Office document types; and compatibility with the older versions of applications.

8 Microsoft Office

9 Ribbon Technology

10 What's Needed

11 Installing Microsoft Office

12 Start an Application

14 Application Start

15 The Application Window

16 Your OneDrive

18 Live Preview

19 Working with the Ribbon

20 Quick Access Toolbar

21 Office Document Types

22 File Extensions

23 Compatibility Mode

24 Convert to the Latest Office Format

Microsoft Office

Microsoft Office is a suite of productivity applications that share common features and approaches. There are two versions: Microsoft Office for one-time purchase, and Microsoft 365 on a regularly updated subscription basis.

There are various retail editions of Microsoft Office:

Office Home & Student edition contains:

- Excel — Spreadsheet and data manager
- PowerPoint — Presentations and slide shows
- Word — Text editor and word processor

Office Home & Business edition contains all of the apps in the Home & Student edition, plus:

- Outlook — Electronic mail and calendar

Office Professional edition contains all applications found in the Home & Business edition, plus two additional apps:

- Access — Database manager
- Publisher — Professional document creation

Similarly, Microsoft 365 has various subscription editions:

Microsoft 365 Personal edition contains all the apps (Excel, PowerPoint, Word, Outlook, Access and Publisher) for one individual – licensed for 1 PC, 1 tablet, and 1 phone.

Microsoft 365 Home edition also contains all the apps, but for an entire household – licensed for 5 PCs, 5 tablets, and 5 phones.

Microsoft 365 Business edition has all apps except Access, plus:

- OneDrive for Business — Online file storage and sharing

Microsoft 365 Business Premium edition contains all the apps found in Microsoft 365 Business (including OneDrive), plus these:

- Microsoft Exchange — Hosted messaging solution
- SharePoint Online — Collaboration web services
- Skype for Business — Hosted communications service

Microsoft 365 Enterprise editions contain all applications found in Microsoft 365 Business Premium edition but also provide additional security and information management tools.

Microsoft Office suite is available for a one-time payment and based on the same applications as the subscription version – **Microsoft 365** (formally named **Office 365**).

OneNote for Windows 10 is now the default, and an Office version of OneNote is no longer included in Office or Microsoft 365. You can still use the previous OneNote 2016 if you desire.

Office Online (see pages 228-229) provides free web-based versions of the common apps, and Office Education provides special features designed for schools, teachers, and students.

Ribbon Technology

Whichever edition of Office or Microsoft 365 that you have, the applications they provide will all feature the graphical user interface based on the Ribbon. This replaced the menus and toolbars that were the essence of earlier versions of Office.

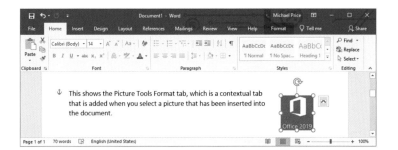

This shows the Ribbon in Word 2019, with the Home tab selected. This tab displays five groups associated with basic document creation – Clipboard, Font, Paragraph, Styles, Editing. Each group contains a set of related commands and icons. Additional contextual tabs appear when appropriate.

The Ribbon contains command buttons and icons, organized in a set of tabs, each containing groups of commands associated with specific functions. The purpose is to make the relevant features more intuitive, and more readily available. This allows you to concentrate on the tasks you want to perform, rather than the details of how you will carry out the activities. Some tabs appear only when certain objects are selected. These are known as contextual tabs, and provide functions that are specific to the selected object. For example, when you select an inserted image, the **Picture Tools**, **Format** tab and its command groups are displayed.

This shows the Picture Tools Format tab, which is a contextual tab that is added when you select a picture that has been inserted into the document.

The Ribbon interface also provides extended ScreenTips that can contain text, images, and links to more help. The tips display as you move the mouse pointer over an option, and describe the functions or give keyboard shortcuts. For example, move the pointer over the Chart command on the Insert tab.

Hot tip

This result-oriented user interface was first introduced in Office 2007, and now appears in all the applications in Office.

Hot tip

For systems with touch-enabled monitors, Office offers a **Touch Mode** ribbon with larger and more widely spaced icons (see page 14).

9

What's Needed

To use Microsoft Office or Microsoft 365, you will need at least the following components in your computer:

- 1GHz processor (32-bit or 64-bit).

- 2GB RAM memory.

- 3GB available disk space.

- 1280 × 800 or larger resolution monitor.

- DirectX 10 graphics card.

- Any edition of Windows 10 or Windows Server 10.

Some functions will have additional requirements; for example:

- Touch-enabled monitor for controlling the system.

- Internet connection for online help.

- CD-ROM or DVD drive for installation, backup and data storage purposes.

Since your computer is required to run a version of Windows 10, the system specifications should meet and exceed the requirements for Microsoft Office or Microsoft 365.

These are the minimum requirements. A higher-speed processor with additional memory will produce faster results.

These system properties are for the PC used in this book, which is running Windows 10 Pro. However, the tasks and topics covered will generally apply to any supported operating system environment.

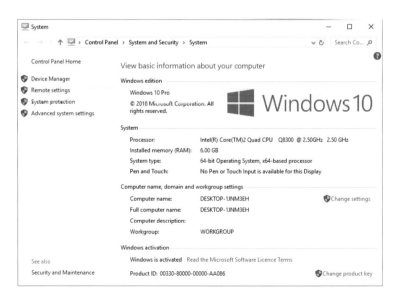

Installing Microsoft Office

You can buy your preferred version of Microsoft Office in disk format from a retail source, or download it directly from an online supplier or from Microsoft itself. However, Windows 10 provides the Office app on the Start menu. This checks the current status of Office on your system. If Office is not already installed, you'll be offered the opportunity to take on a one-month trial of Microsoft 365. This is the subscription-based version of Microsoft Office. When this trial ends, you can commit to a subscription for Microsoft 365 to work across multiple devices or choose the Microsoft 365 Personal version, which lets you use Office on one PC, one tablet, and one phone. This also gives you a massive 1TB of storage for one user.

To compare the editions of Office and Microsoft 365, visit **products. office.com/en-us/buy/ compare-microsoft- office-products**, where you can also try or buy the products.

 Click the **Office** Start menu tile or All Apps entry to check your Office status

If Office is not installed, choose **Install Office** and follow the prompts to begin the installation

Microsoft is eager to encourage adoption of the subscription versions – Microsoft 365 Personal edition also includes 60 minutes per month of Skype calls to cell phones and landlines.

When the install completes, you can explore the Office applications added

Start an Application

With Microsoft Office installed under Windows 10, you can use the Windows 10 Start menu to launch an Office application. For example, to start PowerPoint:

In Tablet or Full Screen mode, select Start then click the All Apps button to show the All Apps list.

1 Select the Start button to display the All Apps list

2 Scroll the alphabetic listing to the **P** heading

3 Choose the **PowerPoint** entry to launch the PowerPoint application

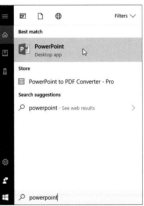

To locate the application more quickly, use the Search box on the Taskbar:

1 Click in the Search box on the Taskbar

2 Begin typing the application name; e.g. powerpoint

3 Click the **PowerPoint** desktop app entry to launch the PowerPoint application

For even quicker access to the Office applications, add tiles to the Start menu:

You can also right-click the desktop app in your Search results to choose to **Pin to Start** (or to choose **Pin to taskbar**).

1 Locate an Office application such as PowerPoint using the All Apps list as described above

2 Right-click the application entry and select **Pin to Start**, typing the application name; e.g. powerpoint

3 Repeat this procedure for each Office application

...cont'd

4 Click Start to display the Start menu, resize and arrange the Office application tiles, and provide a group name

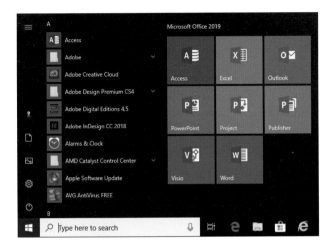

Hot tip

You can resize desktop app tiles as Medium or Small, but the Wide and Large options are not available.

5 Now, to launch an Office application, select Start and click the appropriate tile

You can place icons on the Taskbar for the applications you use most frequently.

1 Right-click the application entry on the All Apps list, and select **More**, then **Pin to taskbar**

2 Repeat this procedure for any other frequently used Office application

3 Your frequently used applications will now be available by simply clicking an icon on the Taskbar

Beware

If you have a microphone and Voice Recognition enabled on your system, you can command Cortana to launch an application, by saying, for example, "Hey Cortana. Start PowerPoint".

13

Application Start

Don't forget

Document-based Office applications open at the Start screen with the **Recent** list and various document templates.

① Select an Office application item such as Word, using any of the methods described on pages 12-13, to display that application's Start screen

Hot tip

The Touch/Mouse Mode button appears by default when you have a touch-enabled monitor. To add it if not displayed, click the Customize Quick Access Toolbar button and then select Touch/Mouse Mode. You can then display the enlarged Ribbon on a standard monitor.

② Select **Blank document** to begin a new editing session with an empty document

③ Click the Touch/Mouse Mode button on the Quick Access Toolbar, and then select 'Touch

④ The expanded Ribbon is displayed, with extra space between the icons and commands, making them easier to select by touch

The Application Window

When you start an Office application such as Excel, PowerPoint or Word, the program window is displayed with a blank document named "Book1", "Presentation1", or "Document1" respectively. Using Word as an example, parts of the application window include:

Backstage (File tab) Quick Access Toolbar Document name Tabs

"Tell Me" Help box
Ribbon Display options

Minimize/Restore/Close

Ribbon Command icons (display lists or galleries)

Collapse the Ribbon

Group launch button (shows dialog box)

Vertical scroll area

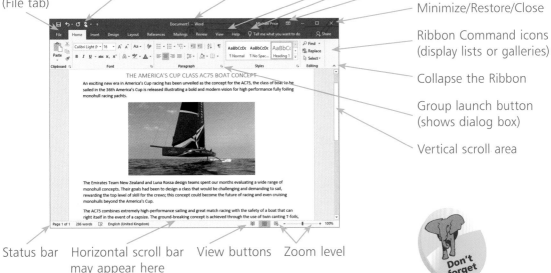

Status bar Horizontal scroll bar may appear here View buttons Zoom level

When you have updated your document and want to save your progress so far, click **File** to display the Backstage command screen and then select **Save** to name and save the document. You can save it in your OneDrive (see page 16) or on your computer.

The **Tell Me** Help box is available in Word, Excel, Outlook, and PowerPoint.

File commands Browse the selected location Save locations Recent folders

From Backstage you can select **Info** for details about your document, or **New** to start another document, or **Open** to display an existing document. There are also printing and sharing options provided.

15

Your OneDrive

To save documents to your OneDrive online storage:

1 Select **File**, **Save As**, then click the OneDrive button

OneDrive was previously known as SkyDrive. When you set up a Microsoft Account to sign in to Windows, you are assigned an allowance of up to 5GB online storage, which is managed on the Microsoft OneDrive server (see also page 228). A Microsoft 365 subscription gives you a further 1TB of storage *(correct at the time of printing)*.

2 Confirm or amend the document name, then choose the appropriate folder (e.g. Office2019) and click **Open**

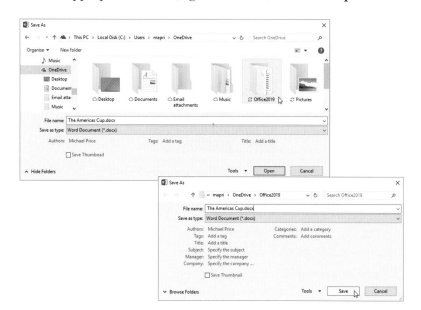

3 Click **Save** to upload the document and save it to your OneDrive folder

4 To access your OneDrive from a browser, go online to **onedrive.live.com**, and sign in if prompted

OneDrive lets you access and edit your documents from any computer where you sign in with the same Microsoft Account. You can also access your OneDrive and documents from a web browser.

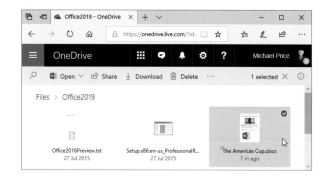

...cont'd

If you have a new system, or have just updated to Windows 10, you may be required to configure OneDrive.

 Select OneDrive and if asked to set up OneDrive, enter your Microsoft Account email and click **Sign in**

By default, the local copies of your OneDrive files will be stored in your personal folder on your hard drive, though you can change the location during setup.

2 Enter your Microsoft Account password, and follow the prompts to complete the setup

3 Click **Open my OneDrive folder** to see the initial features

The files on your OneDrive can be online, and downloaded when needed and flagged as Available. You can mark important files as Always keep on this device.

To start with, you'll have a Documents folder and a Pictures folder, plus an advisory document. You can create more folders, and these will be synced with your online OneDrive and accessible from any device where you sign in with your Microsoft Account.

Live Preview

With the Ribbon interface, you can immediately see the full effect of format options, such as fonts and styles, on your document by simply pointing to the proposed change. For example, to see font formatting changes:

 Highlight the text that you may wish to change, then select the **Home** tab

In earlier versions, you would be shown a preview of the new font or style using a small amount of sample text. Office now displays full previews.

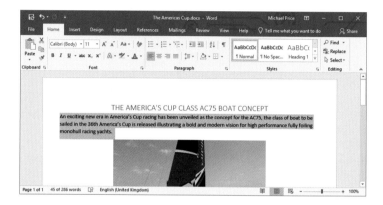

The selected text is temporarily altered to show the font (or the font size, color or highlight) you point to.

 Click the arrow next to the **Font** box and move the mouse pointer over the fonts you'd like to preview

 Click the font you want to apply to the text, or press **Esc** to close the options

 Similarly, you can preview Text Effects, Highlight Colors and Font Colors

Working with the Ribbon

The Ribbon takes up a significant amount of the window space, especially when you have a lower-resolution display. To hide it:

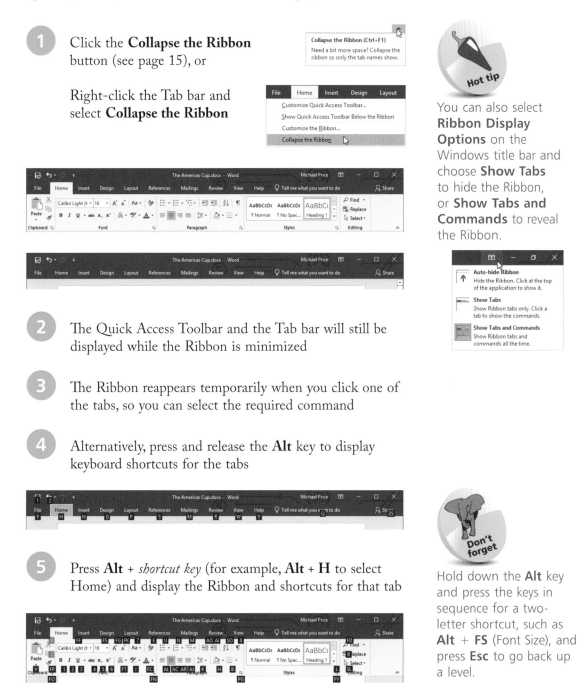

1 Click the **Collapse the Ribbon** button (see page 15), or

Right-click the Tab bar and select **Collapse the Ribbon**

2 The Quick Access Toolbar and the Tab bar will still be displayed while the Ribbon is minimized

3 The Ribbon reappears temporarily when you click one of the tabs, so you can select the required command

4 Alternatively, press and release the **Alt** key to display keyboard shortcuts for the tabs

5 Press **Alt** + *shortcut key* (for example, **Alt** + **H** to select Home) and display the Ribbon and shortcuts for that tab

Hot tip

You can also select **Ribbon Display Options** on the Windows title bar and choose **Show Tabs** to hide the Ribbon, or **Show Tabs and Commands** to reveal the Ribbon.

Don't forget

Hold down the **Alt** key and press the keys in sequence for a two-letter shortcut, such as **Alt** + **FS** (Font Size), and press **Esc** to go back up a level.

Quick Access Toolbar

The Quick Access Toolbar contains a set of commands that are independent of the selected tab. There are five buttons initially:

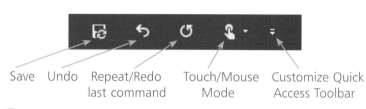

Save   Undo   Repeat/Redo   Touch/Mouse   Customize Quick
                last command   Mode   Access Toolbar

Hot tip

You can right-click any command on the Ribbon and select **Add to Quick Access Toolbar**.

Add to Quick Access Toolbar
Customize Quick Access Toolbar...
Show Quick Access Toolbar Below the Ribbon
Customize the Ribbon...
Collapse the Ribbon

1 Click the **Save** button to save the current contents of the document to your OneDrive, or to the drive on your PC

2 Click **Repeat** to carry out the last action again, or click **Undo** to reverse the last action, and click again to reverse the previous actions in turn

Hot tip

The **Save As** dialog will open the first time you press the **Save** button for a new document.

3 When you have pressed **Undo**, the **Repeat** button changes to become the **Redo** button, which will re-apply in turn the actions that you have reversed

Customize Quick Access Toolbar
New
Open
✓ Save
Email
Quick Print
Print Preview and Print
Spelling & Grammar
Read Aloud
✓ Undo
✓ Redo
Draw Table
✓ Touch/Mouse Mode
More Commands...
Show Below the Ribbon

4 Click the **Customize** button to add or remove icons, using the shortlist of frequently referenced commands

5 Click **More Commands...** to display the full list of commands, then add and remove entries as desired

Don't forget

You can also click the **File** tab, then select the application **Options** and select **Quick Access Toolbar** to display this dialog box.

Word Options
General
Display
Proofing
Save
Language
Ease of Access
Advanced
Customize Ribbon
Quick Access Toolbar
Add-ins
Trust Center

Customize the Quick Access Toolbar.

Choose commands from:
Popular Commands

<Separator>
Accept Revision
Add a Hyperlink
Add Table
Align Left
Bullets
Center
Change List Level
Choose a Text Box

Add >>
<< Remove

Customize Quick Access Toolbar:
For all documents (default)

Save
Undo
Redo
Touch/Mouse Mode

Modify...

Show Quick Access Toolbar below the Ribbon

Customizations: Reset ▼
Import/Export ▼

OK   Cancel

Office Document Types

The files you create using the Office applications will be office documents of various types, including:

- **Word document** — Formatted text and graphics
- **Publisher publication** — Flyers and brochures
- **Excel worksheet** — Spreadsheets and data lists
- **PowerPoint presentation** — Presentations and slide shows

Each item will be a separate file. Typically, these may be saved in your OneDrive Documents folder (or locally on your computer).

1 To review your files, open File Explorer and select your OneDrive Documents folder

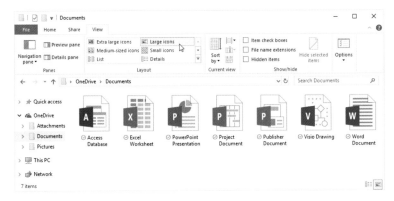

Hot tip

You can specify another folder or sub-folder to organize particular sets of documents.

2 This shows each file as a large icon plus name and OneDrive status. For other styles, click the **View** tab and select, for example, **Details**, to show additional file information such as date modified, type and size

Name	Status	Date modified	Type	Size
Access Database	⊘	25/08/2018 09:47	Microsoft Access Database	484 KB
Excel Worksheet	⊘	25/08/2018 09:50	Microsoft Excel Worksheet	7 KB
PowerPoint Presentation	⊘	25/08/2018 09:58	Microsoft PowerPoint Presentation	280 KB
Project Document	⊘	25/08/2018 09:49	Microsoft Project Document	176 KB
Publisher Document	⊘	25/08/2018 09:49	Microsoft Publisher Document	59 KB
Visio Drawing	⊘	25/08/2018 09:58	Microsoft Visio Drawing	18 KB
Word Document	⊘	25/08/2018 10:05	Microsoft Word Document	13 B

Don't forget

Right-click the header line for Details, and you can select other file attributes such as Date created, Authors, Dimensions, etc.

File Extensions

To see the file extensions that are associated with the various document types:

1 In File Explorer, select the **View** tab and in the **Show/Hide** section of the Ribbon click the box labeled **File name extensions**. Select **Hidden items** also, if you want to check if there are any hidden files in your folder

View
☐ Item check boxes
☑ File name extensions
☑ Hidden items

2 View the contents of your OneDrive Documents folder

3 The file extension will be shown alongside the file name, whichever folder view you choose; e.g. in Details view

Compatibility Mode

Office will open documents created in previous versions of Office applications; for example **.doc** (Word) or **.xls** (Excel).

1 Click the **File** tab and select **Open**, then **Browse**. Choose your Documents folder then click the Down arrow to display the list of document types supported

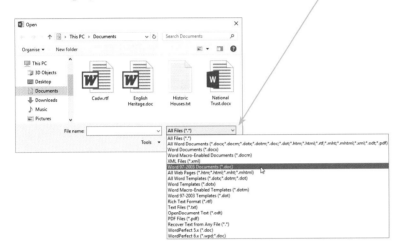

2 Choose the document type (**Word 97-2003** for example) then select a specific file (e.g. **English Heritage.doc**)

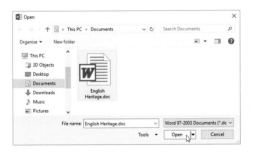

3 Documents created in previous versions (including **.docx** files from Word 2010) are opened in Compatibility Mode

Convert to the Latest Office Format

If you have opened a document in Compatibility Mode, you can convert it to the latest Office format.

Hot tip

You can also click the **File** tab, select **Save As**, and choose the standard Office format (e.g. Word Document) to carry out the conversion.

Beware

Converting will create a file of the same name, but with the latest Office format extension. The original file will be deleted.

Don't forget

With **Save As**, you have the option to change the file name, and the location for the new document.

1 Select the **File** tab and **Info**, then the **Convert** button

2 Click **OK** to confirm, and the file type will be amended

3 To replace the original file, select **File** and then **Save** – see the file extension change in the Word title bar to the new **.docx** file type

4 To retain the original while creating a new file in the latest Office format, you'd select **File**, **Save As**, and then click the **Save** button

2 Create Word Documents

This covers the basics of word processing, using the Word application in Office. It covers entering, selecting and copying text; saving and autosaving; and proofing the text. It looks at the use of styles to structure the document, and adding document features such as pictures, columns, and word counts. It also discusses ways of creating tables, the use of Paste Special, and the facilities for printing.

26   Create a Word Document

27   Enter Text

28   Select and Copy Text

30   Save the Document

31   Correct Proofing Errors

32   Change Proofing Settings

33   Apply Styles

34   Outline View

36   Insert a Picture

38   Page Layout

39   Display in Columns

40   Word Count

41   Create a Table

42   Convert Text to Table

43   Paste Special

44   Print Document

Create a Word Document

There are several ways to create a Word document:

 Right-click any empty space on the Desktop and select **New, Microsoft Word Document** from the context menu that appears

Hot tip

A new right-click document, as shown in Step 1, will be named **New Microsoft Word Document**, though you can rename this to be more relevant by right-clicking on the title and overtyping it. It will appear as an icon on the Desktop.

New Microsoft Word Document.docx

Double-click the file icon to open the document.

Start Word and select **Blank document** (see page 14) to create a document temporarily named "Document1"

If Word is open with an existing document, you can select the **File** tab, click **New**, and choose **Blank document** to create another document

Enter Text

1 Click on the page and type the text that you want. If the text is longer than a single line, Word automatically starts the new line for you

You can copy and paste text from other sources, such as web pages. Use **Paste Options** (see page 29) to avoid copying styles and formats along with the text.

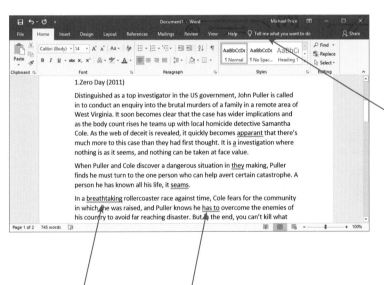

2 Press **Enter** when you need to insert a blank line or start a new paragraph

Select the **Tell Me** tab to see a **Recently Used** drop-down list appear, showing the last five commands you used.

3 Red (spelling) or blue (grammar and style) wavy underlines may appear – to indicate "proofing errors"

4 Click the button on the status bar to correct them one by one, or you can correct proofing errors all at the same time, when you've finished typing the whole document (see page 31)

You may see blue wavy underscores to indicate contextual spelling errors (misused words), such as "Their" in place of "There".

Select and Copy Text

In Word, there are numerous ways to select the portion of text you require, using the mouse or the keyboard, as preferred. To select the entire document, use one of these options:

 Select the **Home** tab, click **Select** in the Editing group, and then click the **Select All** command

 Move the mouse pointer to the left of any text until it turns into a right–pointing arrow, then triple-click

 Press the shortcut keys **Ctrl** + **A** to select all of the text

There are many mouse and keyboard options for selecting a piece of text in the body of the document. For example:

 Double-click anywhere in a word to select it

 Hold down **Ctrl** and click anywhere in a sentence to select the whole sentence

To select a portion of text, click at the start, hold down the left mouse button and drag the pointer over the text, then release the button when the whole section of required text is selected

You can use text selection in combination with the Clipboard tools, to copy or move multiple pieces of text in the same operation. For example:

 1 Select the first section of required text using the mouse to highlight it

You can use the keyboard shortcuts **Ctrl** + **C** (copy), **Ctrl** + **X** (cut), and **Ctrl** + **V** (paste) instead of the Clipboard buttons, as well as right-clicking and selecting options from the context menu.

2 Hold down the **Ctrl** key and select additional pieces of text

3 Select **Home** and click the **Copy** button in the Clipboard group

Click the **Cut** button if you want to move the text rather than copy it.

4 Click the position in the document where the text is required, then select **Home** and click the **Paste** button

Click the arrow below the **Paste** button, then click **Paste Options** and choose between **Keep Source Formatting**, **Merge Formatting**, and **Keep Text Only**.

5 If you've copied several pieces of text, when you paste the selections each piece will appear on a separate line, so you'd need to delete the end-of-line characters and perhaps add spaces, if you want to join them together

Save the Document

When you are building a document, Word will periodically save a copy of the document, just in case a problem arises. This minimizes the amount of text you may need to re-enter if a document is lost, accidentally deleted or becomes corrupt. This feature is known as "AutoRecover". To check the settings:

 Click the **File** tab, select **Options**, then the **Save** command

Beware

If the system terminates abnormally, any data entered since the last AutoRecover operation will be lost.

By default, Word will save AutoRecover information every 10 minutes, but you can change the frequency using the settings in the Word Options screen above.

To make an immediate save of your document:

 Click the **Save** button on the Quick Access Toolbar

Don't forget

You can also select **File**, **Save As**, to specify a new location, name, or document type.

2 The first time, you'll be prompted to confirm the location, the file name, and the document type that you want to use

 On subsequent saves, the document on the hard disk will be updated immediately, without further interaction

Correct Proofing Errors

When you've entered all the text, you can correct proofing errors.

1 Press **Ctrl + Home** to go to the start of the document, select the **Review** tab, then choose **Spelling & Grammar**

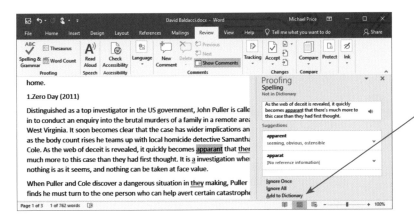

2 The first proofing error is found – a grammar error. Click the **Change** button to accept the offered suggestion, or click the **Ignore** button to decline the suggestion

3 The next proofing error is found – a spelling error. Click the **Change** button or **Ignore** button as preferred, or
Click the **Change All** button or **Ignore All** button to correct all occurrences in the document

The **Spelling & Grammar** check will begin from the current typing cursor location unless you move it to the start of the document. Ensure that the appropriate language dictionary is enabled! (See pages 130-131.)

You can use **Smart Lookup** to find a definition or description of the highlighted text. However, on some systems, this feature is in **Reference**, **Research**.

Use **Add to Dictionary** to add a correct but error-raising word to the dictionary if it is likely to occur often in your documents, and it will not be reported as an error in future.

Change Proofing Settings

 Select the **File** tab, then **Word Options** and **Proofing**

Word Options

General	Change how Word corrects and formats text as you type: [AutoCorrect Options...]
Display	
Proofing	**When correcting spelling in Microsoft Office programs**
Save	☑ Ignore words in UPPERCASE
Language	☑ Ignore words that contain numbers
Ease of Access	☑ Ignore Internet and file addresses
Advanced	☑ Flag repeated words
	☐ Enforce accented uppercase in French
Customize Ribbon	☐ Suggest from main dictionary only
Quick Access Toolbar	[Custom Dictionaries...]
Add-ins	French modes: Traditional and new spellings
Trust Center	Spanish modes: Tuteo verb forms only

[OK] [Cancel]

You can make changes to the settings for the spelling checks, and also for the grammar and style checks.

2 Some settings, such as **Ignore words in UPPERCASE** and **Flag repeated words**, apply to all Office applications

Word Options

General	**When correcting spelling and grammar in Word**
Display	
Proofing	☑ Check spelling as you type
Save	☑ Mark grammar errors as you type
Language	☑ Frequently confused words
Ease of Access	☑ Check grammar with spelling
Advanced	☐ Show readability statistics
	Writing Style: Grammar & Refinements [Settings...]

[OK] [Cancel]

3 Some proofing options are specific to the particular Office application; e.g. Word's **Mark grammar errors as you type**

If you'd rather not use the grammar checker, clear the boxes for **Mark grammar errors as you type** and **Check grammar with spelling**. Alternatively, you can hide errors in that particular document.

4 Some options are specific to the document being worked on

[Recheck Document]

Exceptions for: David Baldacci.docx

☐ Hide spelling errors in this document only
☐ Hide grammar errors in this document only

5 The spell checker in Word is contextual, identifying words that are spelled correctly but used inappropriately, and suggesting more suitable alternatives

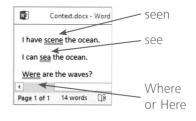

Context.docx - Word — seen

I have scene the ocean. — see

I can sea the ocean.

Were are the waves? — Where or Here

Page 1 of 1   14 words

Apply Styles

 1 Select the **Home** tab, then click in the main heading and select the style for **Heading 1** for major emphasis

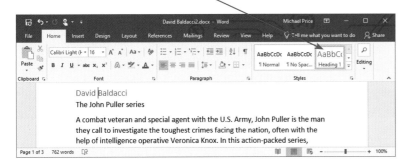

You can change the style for parts of the text to suit the particular contents, using the Styles group on the **Home** tab.

2 Click inside one of the subsidiary headings and select the style for **Heading 2** for minor emphasis

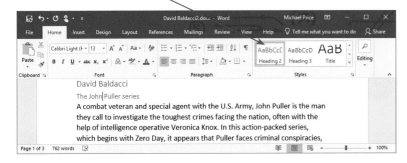

 3 Click within one of the text paragraphs and select the style for **No Spacing** to condense the paragraph

Apply these two styles to other headings and paragraphs. To repeat a style, select an example, double-click the Format Painter icon, and then click each similar item in turn.

4 Click the Down arrow to explore other styles

Outline View

When you have structured the document using headings, you can view it as an outline:

1 Select the **View** tab and click the **Outline** button, to switch to Outline view and enable the **Outlining** tab

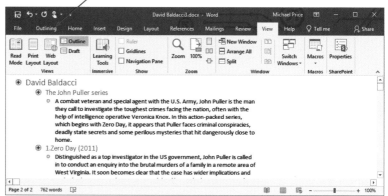

The **Outlining** tab is not enabled by default, so is not visible until it is enabled by the View tab's **Outline** button.

2 In the **Outlining** tab's Outline Tools group, click the box labeled **Show First Line Only** to see more entries

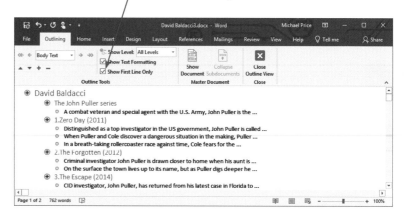

Hot tip

Uncheck the **Show Text Formatting** box to display the entries in plain text, to further increase the number of entries that can be shown.

This makes it easier for you to review the whole document. You might decide that you want to try a different sequence – for example, in an alphabetic order rather than chronologically by date of publication. Using the Outline view makes it easy to reposition the entries to suit your requirements.

...cont'd

1 Click the arrow next to **Show Level**, and choose "Level 2"

2 Click the ⊕ button beside an item to select it. For example, click to select "Contents List" item

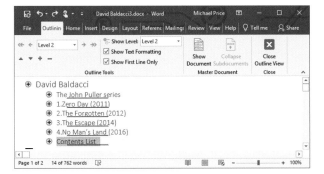

3 Now, click the Up arrow button in the Outline Tools group, and the selected entry, with all its subsidiary levels and text, will move one row for each click on the button

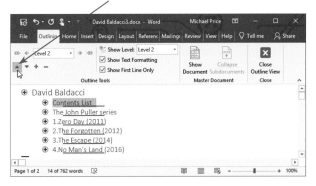

4 Select an item then click the Down arrow in the Outline Tools group to move an entry lower in the list

5 Repeat this procedure to reposition other entries in the list, if appropriate to your need – for example, to sort the book titles alphabetically

This will display the selected level, and all the higher levels in the outline of the document.

You can also click the ⊕ button beside the entry to select it, and then drag it up or down to the required position.

The Outline Tools group also provides buttons that allow you to promote or demote selected entries.

Insert a Picture

 1 Position the typing cursor at the location where you want to add a picture, inserting a blank line if desired

With Word, you can also insert online pictures and video directly without having to download and save them on your computer.

You can insert a variety of items into your document, including pictures; tables; headers and footers; WordArt; and symbols.

 2 Select the **Insert** tab and click the appropriate icon or command; e.g. **Picture** (in the Illustrations group)

Don't forget

The picture will be added to the document, in line with the text. Note the addition of the **Picture Tools, Format** tab.

3 Switch to the appropriate folder and select the file for the required picture and click the **Insert** button

…cont'd

You can adjust the position of the picture on the page of text.

1 Click the **Position** button in the **Format** tab's Arrange group and move the mouse pointer over the buttons

The **Format** tab allows you to change the size, select a frame, and adjust the brightness, contrast, and color of the picture.

2 A live preview will be displayed. Click the appropriate button for the position you prefer

3 Click the Up or Down arrow on the height, to adjust the size of the picture – and you'll see that the width automatically gets changed in proportion to the adjusted height you choose

The original proportions of the picture will be maintained when you make changes to the height or width.

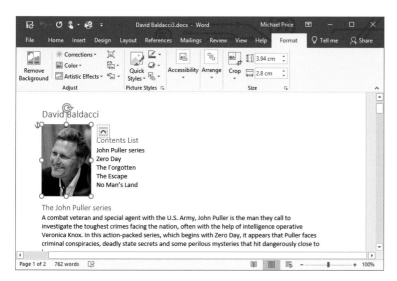

Having chosen the layout, you can select the picture to drag it and make fine adjustments.

Page Layout

The **Layout** tab allows you to control how the document contents are placed on the page, by just clicking one of the function command buttons in the Page Setup group.

To display the vertical and horizontal rulers, as shown here, select the **View** tab and then click the **Ruler** box, from the Show group.

1 Click the **Orientation** button to select **Portrait** or **Landscape**

2 Click the **Size** button to select the paper size from the list, or click **More Paper Sizes...** to show other choices, including **Custom size**

You can also press the arrowed group button in the Page Setup group to display the **Page Setup** dialog.

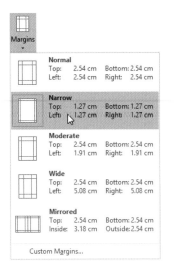

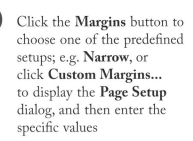

3 Click the **Margins** button to choose one of the predefined setups; e.g. **Narrow**, or click **Custom Margins...** to display the **Page Setup** dialog, and then enter the specific values

Display in Columns

1 Select the text to put into columns and click the **Layout** tab, then select **Columns** from the Page Setup group

Hot tip

Leave all of the text unselected if you wish to apply the columns to the whole document.

2 Choose the number of columns required; e.g. **Three**

3 Click in the body text; select the **Home** tab; click **Select**; **Select Text with Similar Formatting**; and click the **Justify** button

Hot tip

Choose **Justify** for the paragraph text, to help give the document the appearance of newspaper columns. Choose **Center** for the title text, to place it over the three columns.

Word Count

If you are preparing a document for a publication, such as a club magazine, you may need to keep track of the number of words:

When there is partial text selected, the status bar shows word counts for the selection and the whole document.

Page 1 of 2   12 of 762 words

View the word count for the document on the status bar

Click the word count to display the detailed counts for pages, paragraphs, lines, and characters

For a fuller analysis of the contents of the document:

Select **File**, **Options**, **Proofing**, then **Show readability statistics**

Select the **Review** tab, then click the **Spelling & Grammar** button in the Proofing group for a complete analysis of the document

After the spelling check is completed, the document readability statistics are displayed

You can also display the word count details by selecting the **Review** tab and clicking the **Word Count** button in the Proofing group.

Create a Table

To create a table in your document:

You'll see previews in the document of the indicated table sizes as you move the pointer across the **Insert Table** area.

1 Click the point where you want to add the table, then click the **Insert** tab, and select **Table**

2 Select the desired number of rows and columns, then click to insert the table and type in the contents

Press the **Tab** key to move across columns, or use the arrow keys to navigate around the table. Click and drag a separator line to adjust the width of a column.

Book Number	Title	ISBM	Publication Date
1	Zero Day	0-330-520381	November 2011
2	The Forgotten	0-230-749283	November 2012
3	The Escape	1-447-225362	April 2015
4	No Man's Land		

3 Select the **Design** tab to choose your preferred table style

Convert Text to Table

If you already have the text that's needed for the table, perhaps taken from another document, you can convert the text into a table:

 Make sure that the cell entries are separated by a comma or tab mark, or some other unique character

The cursor must be in the table area to display the **Table Tools** tab. Select its **Layout** tab to see operations such as insert, delete, and align.

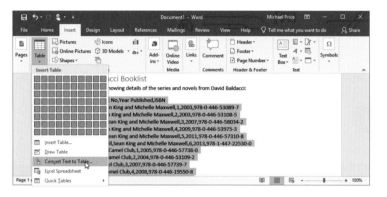

Select **AutoFit to contents**, to adjust the column widths to match the data in those cells.

2 Highlight the text, select the **Insert** tab, and then click **Table**, **Convert Text to Table...**

3 Specify your particular separation character and then click **OK**

 The table will be created with the data inserted into the relevant cells, which may be expanded to hold the data. Select the **Design** tab to explore the table style offered

Select **Home**, then click the **Show/Hide** button in the Paragraph group to display tabs and paragraph marks. Two consecutive commas or tabs indicate an empty cell. Paragraph marks separate the rows.

Paste Special

To copy text without including its formatting and graphics:

1 Highlight the text you want, then right-click the selected area and click the **Copy** command

2 Click in the document where the text is needed, and from the **Home** tab, click the arrow below the **Paste** button

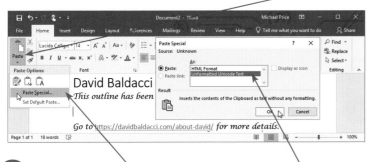

3 Click **Paste Special...** and choose **Paste, Unformatted Unicode Text**

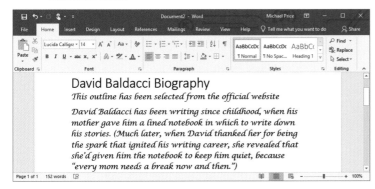

Information copied from other documents or web pages may include graphics, formatting, and colors inappropriate for your document.

Graphical information won't be copied, even if it has the appearance of text (as is sometimes the case with the initial letter of a piece of fancy text).

The copied text will inherit the format of that part of the document you clicked before carrying out the paste operation.

Print Document

 To print your document from within Word, click the **File** tab and select **Print** (or press **Ctrl + P**)

In Office programs, you can preview and print your documents at one location – in the **Print** section of the Backstage area.

You can view the document as it will appear in print by selecting the **View** tab and selecting the **Print Layout** button from the Views group.

 From here, you can use the scroll bars, the zoom slider, and the page change buttons to preview the document

From here, you can use the scroll bars, the zoom slider, and the page change buttons to preview the document

Select the specific printer to use

Choose the page/s to print

Adjust other settings, such as the paper and margin sizes

Specify the number of copies, then click the **Print** button

Quick Print

You can add the **Quick Print** button to the Quick Access Toolbar (see page 14) to get an immediate print of the current document, using the default settings.

3 Complex Documents

Microsoft Word can be used to create and edit more complex documents, such as booklets and brochures. This chapter covers importing text; inserting illustrations; and creating tables of contents and figures. It shows how templates can be used to help create documents, and also introduces Publisher, the Office application that is specifically designed for desktop publishing.

46 Start a Booklet

47 Choose Page Arrangement

48 Create the Structure

50 Import Text

52 Insert Illustrations

53 Add Captions

54 Table of Contents

56 Table of Figures

58 Insert Preface

59 Update Table of Contents

60 Decorate the Page

62 Templates

64 Publisher

65 Create a Publication

66 Print the Publication

Start a Booklet

To illustrate some of the facilities available for creating and organizing complex documents, we'll go through the process of importing and structuring the text for a booklet. Our example uses the text for "A Study in Scarlet" by Sir Arthur Conan Doyle.

1 Start by typing the book title, author, and chapter names

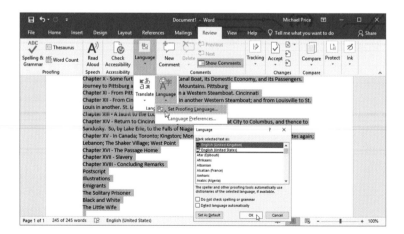

The text for books in the public domain can be found online from websites such as Project Gutenberg at **gutenberg.org**

You need to highlight all the text to change to a different language for the whole document.

2 When you've entered all the chapter headings, set the language. This is a British book, so press **Ctrl + A** to highlight all text; select **Review**, **Language**, **Set Proofing Language...**, **English (United Kingdom)** and click **OK**

3 Click **Save** on the Quick Access Toolbar, and provide a name for the document, or accept the suggested name

Choose Page Arrangement

Now, specify the paper size, the margins and the page style:

 1 Select the page **Layout** tab, and click **Size** to choose the paper size you are printing on; for example, "Letter"

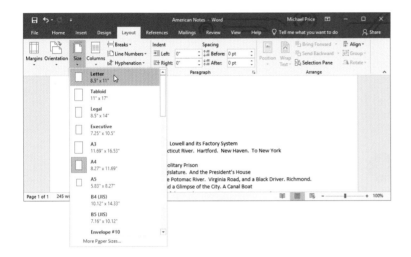

2 Click the group button on the Page Setup group to display the **Page Setup** dialog

3 In the **Pages** section, click the **Multiple pages** arrow button, then select **Book fold** from the drop-down menu

4 Click the **Sheets per booklet** arrow button, then select **4** from the drop-down menu

You can specify the number of sheets in multiples of 4 up to 40, to assemble the document in blocks of pages, or choose **All** to assemble the document as a single booklet.

Front

Back

Create the Structure

1 Highlight the text for the chapter titles

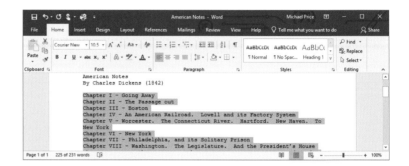

Don't forget

This particular book has two parts, with seven chapters in each part.

2 Click the **Home** tab and select **Styles**, **Heading 1**

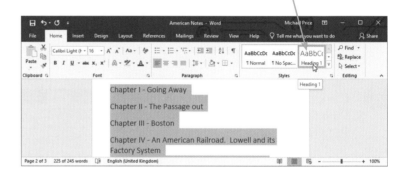

3 With the chapter titles still selected, click the **Center** button in the Paragraph group

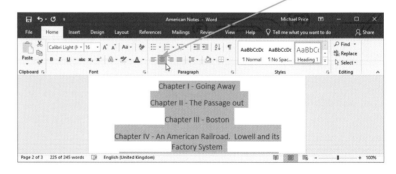

Don't forget

The formatting changes center the chapter titles over the text that will be inserted (see page 50).

4 To replace hyphens with line breaks in the chapter titles, click the Editing group's **Replace** button, to open the **Find and Replace** dialog

5 In the **Find what** box, type a hyphen with a space either side; i.e. " - " (without the quotation marks)

6 In the **Replace with** box, type the "^l" (carat, lowercase L) control code for a line break, then click **Replace All**

7 This changes all the occurrences in the selected text. Click **No** to skip the remainder of the document, to avoid changing hyphens elsewhere in the text

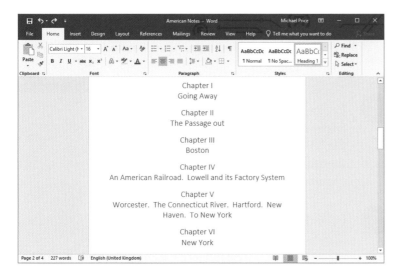

Steps 4 to 6 illustrate how you can use **Find** and **Replace** to insert special characters such as line breaks. You can click the **More** button and select **Special**, **Manual Line Break** to insert the required code.

To see paragraph and line break codes, click the **Show/Hide** button (in the Paragraph group on the **Home** tab).

Chapter·I↵
Going·Away¶

Chapter·II↵
The·Passage·out¶

Note that each title remains a single item, even though spread over two lines.

Import Text

Hot tip

Type paragraphs of text, insert text from a file, or copy and paste text from a file if you just want part of the contents.

Don't forget

This option was known as **Insert File** in earlier versions of Word. It allows you to transfer the contents from various file types, including Word, web, and text.

1 Click immediately to the left of the "Chapter I" title, and select **Insert**, **Page Break** to start the chapter on a new page

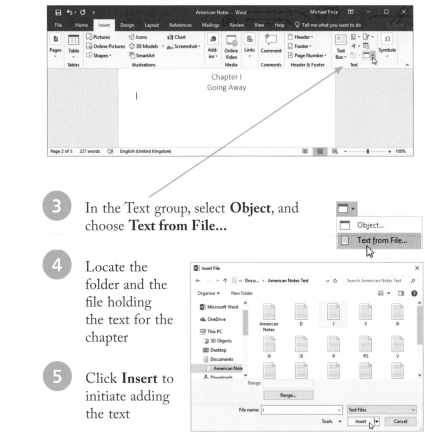

2 Click the page, just past the end of the title, and press **Enter** to add a new blank line in body text style

3 In the Text group, select **Object**, and choose **Text from File...**

4 Locate the folder and the file holding the text for the chapter

5 Click **Insert** to initiate adding the text

6 Click **OK** to select the appropriate encoding, if prompted

The text will be copied to the document at the required location.

Step 6 is only required when the system needs your help in interpreting the imported text.

Repeat Steps 1 to 6 for each chapter in the book.

To adjust the style for the inserted text:

1 Click anywhere in the inserted text; click the **Home** tab; then in the Editing group, click **Select** and choose **Select All Text with Similar Formatting**

2 Select your preferred style (for example, **Normal** or **No Spacing**) plus a Paragraph option such as **Justify**, and all of the inserted text will be converted to those settings

The inserted text may not have the format you require, but you can change all of the inserted text in a single operation to a style that you prefer.

This allows you to adjust the style for all the pieces of text you have inserted, but it does rely on the inserted text having a style that is not used elsewhere in your document.

Insert Illustrations

 Find the location for an illustration. For example, select **Home**, **Find**, and enter a search term, such as "[Picture"

 Select the placeholder text describing the illustration, then choose the **Insert** tab and click **Pictures**

 Locate the file containing the required illustration and click **Insert**, and the picture is inserted into the document, in line with the text

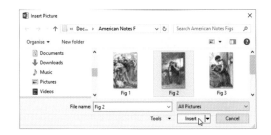

 Adjust its size and its position as required

Add Captions

You can add the descriptive text in the form of a caption that can be managed automatically as you update the document, and maintain a contents list.

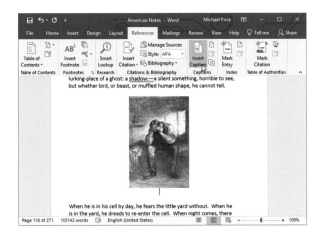

Repeat the steps from these two pages to insert a picture and a caption for each of the figures in the book.

1 From the **References** tab, select **Insert Caption**

2 Click **OK** to accept the automatic number

If the document doesn't already contain the title for the illustration, you can type it after the automatic number in the **Caption** box.

3 Type a colon and a space, then copy or type the text for the picture title to follow after the figure number

4 Click away from the caption to see the figure as it will appear in the final document

Figure 2: The Solitary Prisoner

The captions that you create are used to create a Table of Figures (see pages 56-57).

5 Repeat this procedure for each of the pictures in the document, until you have all the figures and captions

Table of Contents

When you have formatted text within the document with heading levels, you can use these to create and maintain a contents list.

 Select **Home**, **Find**, **Go To**, then select **Page**, **Enter page number** "2", then click **Go To**, **Close** to show that page

You can prefix the number with **+** or **-** to go forward or back for the specified number of pages.

2 Select the **Insert** tab and click **Blank Page** in the Pages group, to insert the blank page where you will add the contents list

3 Go to the new page 2, select the **References** tab, and click the **Table of Contents** button to display the types of tables that are offered

If the typing cursor is centered, select **Home**, then click **Align Text Left** in the Paragraph group, before selecting the **Table of Contents** button.

4 Choose the type of table that you want – for example, **Automatic Table 1** (with "Contents" as the title)

Hot tip

Automatic tables are generated from heading levels 1, 2 and 3. You can also build tables from custom styles, or manually selected text.

5 The Table of Contents is inserted into the document

Beware

The Table of Contents must be updated to show any changes to the heading-text content, or to the page-number value.

6 When you click in the Table of Contents, its entries are grayed, to indicate they are field codes (action items)

Don't forget

When you hover the mouse pointer over an entry in the table, with the Shift key pressed, you'll have a link to the associated section of the document.

Table of Figures

 Go to the start of "Chapter I" and insert another blank page, this time for a list of illustrations

 On the new page, type "Illustrations", then select the **Home** tab and the **Styles group** button, and choose **Heading 1**

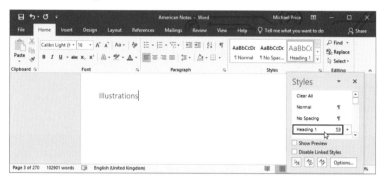

Click the **Insert** tab, then choose **Blank Page** from the Pages group to insert a blank page.

Press **Enter** to add a blank line, then, on the **References** tab, click the **Table of Figures** dialog button – to launch the Table of Figures dialog

Select the **Caption** label – i.e. "Figure" – then check or clear the page number options boxes as desired

Entries for the chosen caption type, in this case "Figure", will be identified and included in the table.

Click **OK** to insert the Table of Figures as shown in the Print Preview

6 The layout for the Table of Figures is similar to that of the Table of Contents created previously

There's no heading included, so any heading required must be provided separately; in this case, "Illustrations".

7 Click the table to see the grayed entries indicating that there are field codes and links to the figures

8 Right-click a table entry and select **Toggle Field Codes** to reveal or hide the field code for that table entry

The format of the field codes for the Table of Figures indicates that it is actually a TOC (Table of Contents) format, but using the "Figure" label.

Insert Preface

 Go to page 2 (the "Contents" page) and insert a blank page for the book Preface

 On the new page, type "Preface", select the **Home** tab then the **Styles group** button, and choose **Heading 1**

 Press **Enter** and insert text from a file (see page 50). Alternatively, type the text for the Preface

 Adjust the formatting and alignment of the text as desired; for example, selecting **Justify** for the main portion

Select **Save** on the Quick Access Toolbar to save the latest changes that you have made

Update Table of Contents

When you make changes, such as to the Preface or the illustrations list, that include new headings (level 1, 2 or 3), the Table of Contents is affected. However, the updates will not be displayed immediately. To apply the updates:

1 Locate the Table of Contents and click anywhere within it

Contents

Chapter I Going Away 3
Chapter II The Passage out 11
Chapter III Boston 26
Chapter IV An American Railroad. Lowell and its Factory System 64
Chapter V Worcester. The Connecticut River. Hartford. New Haven. To New York 73
Chapter VI New York 83
Chapter VII Philadelphia, and its Solitary Prison 102

Hot tip

Whenever you add text to the document, or insert pages, the page numbers for the entries in the Table of Contents change, but the changes will not appear until you explicitly select **Update Table...**.

2 Click **Update Table...** at the top of the table

3 Check **Update entire table** to add new items, and click **OK**

Update Table of Contents

Word is updating the table of contents. Select one of the following options:
- ○ Update page numbers only
- ● Update entire table

OK   Cancel

4 New entries are inserted and the page numbers are updated as appropriate

Contents

Preface 2
Illustrations 4
Chapter I Going Away 6
Chapter II The Passage out 14
Chapter III Boston 29
Chapter IV An American Railroad. Lowell and its Factory System 67
Chapter V Worcester. The Connecticut River. Hartford. New Haven. To New York 76
Chapter VI New York 86

Don't forget

If you've added pages or text to your document, but have not changed the headings, select **Update page numbers only**.

59

Decorate the Page

You can enhance the formatting of the title page using styles or WordArt.

 Select a section of text, expand **Styles**, and move the mouse over the options presented to preview the styles

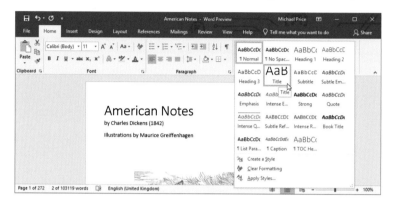

 Click your preferred style to apply that format to the selected text. For example, select the book title and choose the **Title** style. For other selections of text you can choose styles such as **Subtitle** or one of the various other options

Title, centered

Subtitle, centered

Intense Quote

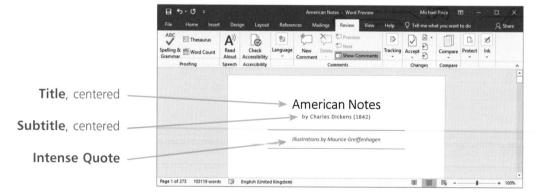

 Select **Center** if desired. Some styles, e.g. **Intense Quote**, are centered by default

 For more impact, select text and choose **WordArt** from the Text group on the **Insert** tab

5 Review the WordArt styles offered and select an option

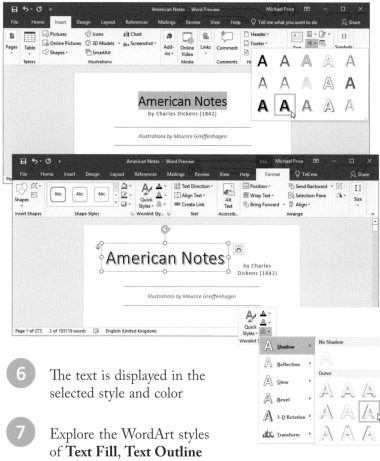

The WordArt effects are not displayed during Insert until you select a specific option. You can select a different option or clear the WordArt if you change your mind.

6 The text is displayed in the selected style and color

7 Explore the WordArt styles of **Text Fill**, **Text Outline** and **Text Effects**, and apply your choice

Full Reflection and **Double Wave Transform** are just two of the options offered in the **Text Effects**.

Templates

When you need a specialized form of document, you can use a predefined document template to help you get started.

 Click the **File** tab, select **New**, and scroll through the featured templates to find one that meets your needs

When you carry out a search, you will see a list of around 20 template categories, with counts of the number of templates in each category. Use this list to refine your searches.

 If there's nothing appropriate among the samples, search for online templates using one of the suggested searches, or provide a suitable search term; e.g. "Greeting Cards"

3 Click the desired template, and click the **Create** button to begin the process of downloading the template

4 When the download completes, a new document based on the downloaded template will be opened

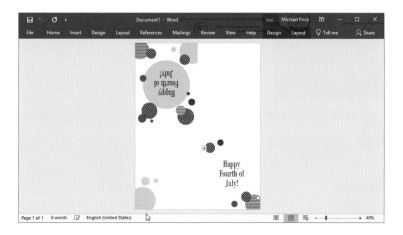

Hot tip

When you download a template, it is added to the list of featured templates, so it is easy to find if you need to access it in the future.

5 Modify the contents of the text boxes to personalize the document, then save the document with an appropriate file name

Hot tip

This template is a four-fold document, and part of the content is inverted so that it appears correctly when folded. Other templates may be two-fold or single sheet.

Publisher

Publisher provides a higher level of desktop publishing capability, with a great variety of paper sizes and styles, including many templates for brochures, leaflets, etc., and lots of guidance.

 Start Publisher, which opens with a selection of document templates

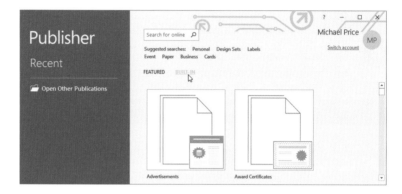

 Explore the **Featured** and **Built-In** templates offered, or search for online templates by topic; e.g. "Birthday"

 Review the selection provided, and select any template to see a detailed description of that design

Create a Publication

1 Choose a template such as "Party invitation" and click the **Create** button to download the template

2 A new document opens, based upon that template

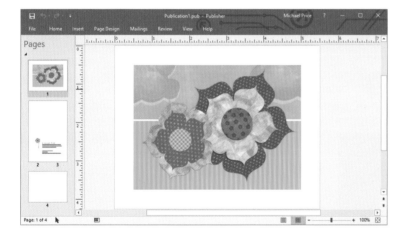

3 Select section 2; enter the title, description and details for the invitation; then save the document

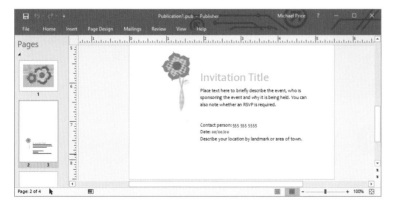

The greeting card is divided into four parts, each one-quarter of the physical page, making it easier to view and edit each part.

Publisher offers various different sizes and layouts of greeting cards; for example:

Print the Publication

 Add any other text or images desired, then save the final version of the document

Publisher shows the pages in a horizontal upright format, but will adjust the orientation of each page when you are ready to print the document.

 Select **File**, **Print**, to see the document as it appears on paper – a single sheet, with sections 2, 3 and 4 inverted

Once printed, the sheet is folded in half, and then folded in half again, to form the greeting card.

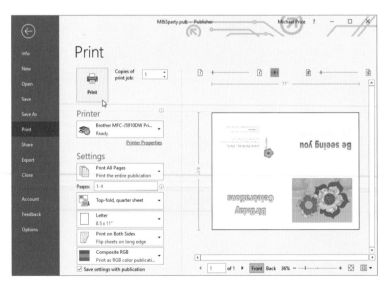

Adjust the settings as required, select the printer that you wish to use, and then click the **Print** button

4 Calculations

This chapter looks at Excel – the spreadsheet application – and covers creating a new workbook, entering data, replicating values, formatting numbers, adding formulas and functions, and using templates.

68 Start Excel

70 Enter Data

72 Quick Fill

74 Sums and Differences

76 Formatting

78 Rounding Up

80 Find a Function

82 Goal Seeking

84 Templates

Start Excel

To start Microsoft Excel with a fresh new spreadsheet, using the temporary name "Book1":

1 Launch the Excel application, using any of the methods described on pages 12 and 13 – via the Start menu, Taskbar icon or Search box, or ask Cortana

2 By default, Excel opens at the Start screen

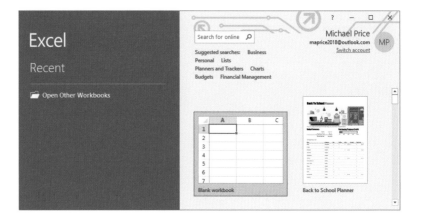

3 From the Excel Start screen, select **Blank workbook** to open an empty spreadsheet called "Book1"

Hot tip

You can have Excel open immediately with the blank document "Book1", bypassing the Start screen. Select **File**, **Options**, **General**, then scroll down to the **Start up Options** section. Now, uncheck the box for **Show Start screen when this application starts** and click **OK**.

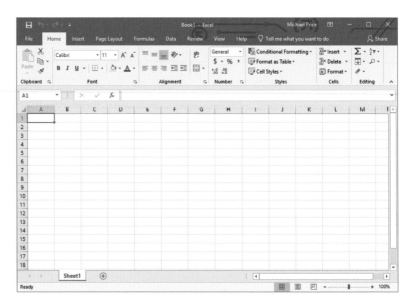

...cont'd

The spreadsheet presented is an Excel workbook that initially contains a single worksheet, which is blank. The cells that it contains are empty – all 17 million of them.

 1 To move to the last row (1048576) in the worksheet, press **End**, and then press the Down arrow key

It may be impractical to utilize even a fraction of the total number of cells available, but the enlarged sheet size does give greater flexibility in designing spreadsheets. For larger amounts of data, you should use Access (see pages 104-105).

2 To move to the last column (XFD) in the worksheet, press **End**, and then press the Right arrow key

If the worksheet contains data, the action taken depends on the initial location of the selected cell.

There can be up to 1048576 rows and 16384 columns. This compares with 65536 rows and 256 columns in some earlier releases.

1 If the selected cell contains data, pressing **End** and then an arrow key takes you to the edge of the data area

2 If the current cell is empty, you move to the start of the adjacent data area

3 If there's no more data in that direction, you'll move to the edge of the worksheet, as with an empty worksheet

Movement is always in the direction of the arrow key you press after pressing the **End** key.

Enter Data

The most common use of spreadsheets is for financial planning; for example, to keep track of business and travel expenditure. To create a family budget:

 1 Open a blank worksheet, select cell A1 and type the title for the spreadsheet; e.g. "Family Budget"

Hot tip

You can find ready-made budget spreadsheets and templates at the Microsoft Office website, and at other internet locations. However, it is useful to create such a spreadsheet from scratch, to illustrate the processes involved.

 2 Press **Enter**, or the down key, to insert the text and move to cell A2, then type the next entry, "Income"

Don't forget

You can change the format of the labels to highlight entries such as Title, Income, and Expenses (see page 76).

 3 Repeat this process to add the remaining labels for the income and expense items that you want to track, and labels for the totals and balance

...cont'd

If you omit an item, you can insert an additional worksheet row. For example, to include a second "Salary" income item:

1 Click a cell (e.g. C4) in the row that's just below where the new entry is required, and select **Insert**, **Insert Sheet Rows** from the Cells group on the **Home** tab

Hot tip

Select a vertical group of cells to insert that many rows above the selected cells. Note that you can insert one or more columns in a similar manner, by selecting **Insert**, **Insert Sheet Columns**.

2 Enter the additional label (for example, "Salary 2nd"), into the cell A4 on the new row

Hot tip

You can also select the cell and press **F2** to make changes to the content of a cell, or select the cell and modify its content on the Formula bar.

3 Double-click an existing cell to edit or retype the entry; for example, to change the existing entry in cell A3 from "Salary" to "Salary 1st"

Quick Fill

You can create one column of data, then let Excel replicate the cell contents for you. For example:

 Enter month and values in column C: "January" in C2 and values in cells C3-C6 and C9-C14, for example

Don't forget

You can widen column A to accommodate the whole text (see the Hot Tip on page 78), then delete column B. To fully explore the data, see page 88.

 Highlight cells C2-C14, then move the mouse pointer over the bottom-right cell until the pointer changes to a **+** Fill handle

3 When the cursor becomes a **+** Fill handle, drag it to the right to replicate the cells for further months

Hot tip

Click in cell C2, hold down the **Shift** key and click in cell C15 to highlight the whole column range of cells.

4 Release the **+** Fill handle when the required number of columns is indicated

Excel detects weekdays to create a series, such as Monday, Tuesday; and it detects abbreviated names, such as Jan, Feb, or Mon, Tue; and so on.

5 Numeric values are duplicated, but the month name is detected and succeeding month names are inserted

After you release the Fill handle, an Auto Fill Options button appears. Click this to control the action – for example, to replicate the formatting only, or to copy cells without devising a series such as Months.

○ Copy Cells
◉ Fill Series
○ Fill Formatting Only
○ Fill Without Formatting
○ Fill Months

Having initialized the cells, you can edit or replace the contents of individual cells to finalize the data.

6 As you enter data into the worksheet, remember to periodically click the Save button on the Quick Access Toolbar

Save As

← → ↑ « Documents › Calculate ∨ Ö Search Calculate 🔎

File name: Family Budget

Save as type: Excel Workbook

Authors: Michael   Tags: Add a tag

☐ Save Thumbnail

∨ Browse Folders   Tools ▾   Save   Cancel

The first time you click the Save button, you'll be prompted to provide a file name in place of the default "Book1".

Sums and Differences

When you've entered the data, and made the changes required, you can introduce functions and formulas to complete the worksheet.

  Click cell C7 (total income for January), then select the **Home** tab, click **Editing** and then Σ **AutoSum** to sum the adjacent values

Numerical cells in the block immediately adjacent to the selected cell will be selected, and included in the **AutoSum** function. Always check that Excel has selected the appropriate cells.

Hot tip

The Ribbon can be collapsed and expanded in Excel, just as it can in Word.

2 Press **Enter** to show the total, then repeat the procedure for cell C15 (total expenses for January)

  Click in cell C16, which is intended for the net balance for January

4 Type =, click C7, type -, then click C15 (to calculate total income minus total expenses for the month of January)

5 Press **Enter** to complete the formula and display the sum

6 Select cell C7 and use the Fill handle to replicate the formula for the other months (February to June), and repeat this process for cells C15 and C16

Formatting

Changing the format for various parts of the worksheet can make it easier to review and assess the results.

1 Click A1 (the title cell), then select the **Home** tab, choose a larger font size, and select a font effect, such as Bold

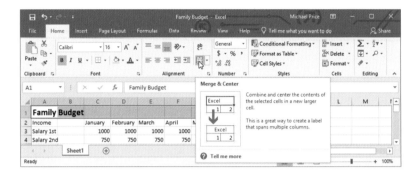

2 Press **Shift**, and click H1 to highlight the row across the data, then click the **Merge & Center** button

You can change each cell individually, or press **Ctrl** and click each of the cells to select them, then apply the changes to all the cells at once.

3 Click the Categories and Totals labels (e.g. A2, A7, A8, A15, A16), and change the font size and effects

4 Or, click **Cell Styles** to pick a suitable style for selected cells

To emphasize the "Net Balance" values for each month:

 1 Select the range of cells; e.g. C16:H16

Excel includes a very useful **Conditional Formatting** facility, where the effects applied depend on the actual contents of the cells being formatted.

2 Select **Styles, Conditional Formatting, Color Scales** and choose one of the swatches. For example, you might select the Green–Yellow–Red color scale

3 The cells are colored and shaded appropriately for the values that they contain

Positive balances are green – the larger the balance, the deeper the shade. Modest balances are yellow, and shades of red are applied to negative balances.

Double-click the separator bar between the A and B headings to extend the column width to fit the longest entry.

Rounding Up

You can use Excel functions such as ROUNDUP or CEILING to adjust the solutions of numerical problems, such as the number of tiles needed to cover the floor area of a room.

1 Open a new, blank worksheet, and enter these labels in the first column:

Number of Tiles
Tile Length
Tile Width
Room Length
Room Width
Number of Tiles
Per Box
Boxes

The number of tiles in cell B6 is the calculated quantity of tiles required to cover the floor space exactly.

2 Enter sample sizes in cells B2:B5, making sure that you use the same units for the tile and room dimensions

3 In cell B6, type the formula **=(B4/B2)*(B5/B3)**

4 In cell B8, type the formula **=B6/B7**

You need to calculate whole numbers of tiles, allowing for wastage where tiles need to be cut to fit.

For these figures, and on the basis of these calculations, you might think 5 boxes would be sufficient. However, if you fit the tiles to the area, you find that some tiles have to be trimmed. The wastage leaves part of the area uncovered.

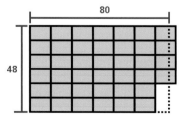

To ensure that there are enough whole tiles to completely cover the area, you need to round up the evaluations:

1 Copy B2:B8 to C2:C8, and, in cell C6, type the formula **=CEILING(C4/C2,1)*CEILING(C5/C3,1)**

The number of whole tiles increases to 42, which will now cover the complete floor area, even after cutting.

This gives 5.25 boxes. Assuming that boxes must be purchased in whole numbers, this result also needs rounding up.

2 Copy C2:C8 to D2:D8, and in cell D8, type the formula **=ROUNDUP(D6/D7,0)** to get the result of 6 boxes

Find a Function

There are a large number of functions available in Excel. They are organized into a library of categories to make it easier to find the particular function you need.

1 Select the **Formulas** tab to show the Function Library

You can click the **More Functions** button to display a secondary list of categories from which to choose.

📊	Statistical ▶
📐	Engineering ▶
📦	Cube ▶
ⓘ	Information ▶
📋	Compatibility ▶
🌐	Web ▶

2 Click a category in the Function Library for an alphabetic list of functions it offers. For example, click the **Logical** category

Logical ▾
- AND
- FALSE
- IF
- IFERROR
- IFNA
- IFS
- NOT
- OR
- SWITCH
- TRUE
- XOR
- *fx* Insert Function...

3 If you don't know where to look for a function you want, click the **Insert Function** button to find a function

4 From Insert Function, type a description of the function you need, in the **Search for a function** box. For example, type "Loan repayment" then press **Go** and choose from the list of recommended functions

5 Alternatively, you can click the arrow button by the **Or select a category** box and choose from the drop-down list of categories, then pick a function from the list offered. For example, choose the "Financial" category

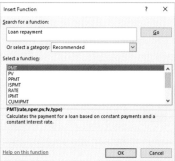

Enter keywords related to the activity you want to perform, and Excel will list all potentially relevant functions.

6 Choose a function, such as the **PMT** function, then click the **OK** button to launch the Function Arguments dialog

The function arguments for the selected function are shown, and a brief description is provided.

7 Type the values for the arguments **Rate** (interest rate per period of loan), **Nper** (number of repayments), and **Pv** (present value of loan amount), then press **OK**

You can optionally provide a final value, **Fv** (the cash balance), and also specify the **Type** (payments made at the start or the end of each period).

8 The function is inserted into the worksheet, and the result is displayed as a negative figure (indicating a payment)

Goal Seeking

Using the **PMT** function, you can establish the monthly payments required to pay off a long-term loan over 25 years, for example.

Hot tip

To calculate payments for an interest-only loan, set **Fv** (see page 81) to the same value as the loan amount.

Suppose, however, you'd like to know how many years it takes to pay off the loan if you increase the payments, let's say, to $1500.

1 One way to establish this is by trial and error, adjusting the number of years until you get the required payment

Don't forget

You would carry on refining your estimate – e.g. trying 12 then 14 – to discover that the correct answer lies between these two periods.

2 Try 20 years, then 15 years, then 10 years, until the payment goes above the $1500 level. This indicates that the appropriate period would be more than 10 years, but less than 15 years

However, Excel provides an automatic way to apply this type of goal-seeking process, and this can give you an exact answer very quickly with a single trial.

...cont'd

 Click the cell containing the function, then select the **Data** tab, and click the **What-If Analysis** button in the Forecast group

Hot tip

Use the **Scenario Manager** to create a set of results for a range of values, such as 10, 15 and 20 years of repayments.

2 Select the **Goal Seek...** option and specify the required result as -1500 (the payment per month) and the change to cell B4 (the number of years for full repayment)

3 **Goal Seek** tries out various values for the changing cell, until the desired solution is found

4 Click **OK** to see the solution appear in the worksheet

Beware

You must specify the target payment as a negative value, since it is a repayment, otherwise **Goal Seek** will be unable to find a solution:

83

Hot tip

You can select a range of data, then click **Forecast Sheet** to generate a quick pop-up forecast.

Templates

 Select the **File** tab and click the **New** button

You can get started with your worksheet by using one of the ready-made templates, which are offered for many common requirements.

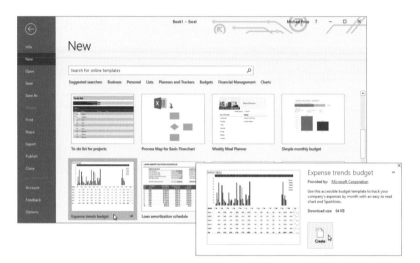

 Select any of the **Featured** templates to view their content, and click **Create** to open a document using the template

 Alternatively, select a category to review the templates from Microsoft Office Online

 Choose a template to see the layout, then click **Create** to download that template and open a document using it

Check periodically to find out which new templates have been added to the Office Online website (www.office.com).

5 Manage Data

Excel also manages data, so we will look at importing data, applying sorts and filters, and selecting specific sets of data. The data can be used to create a chart, or you can arrange the data in tables, insert totals and computations, and look up values. Some editions of Office include Access, which offers full database management functions.

86	Import Data
88	Explore the Data
89	Sort
91	Filters
92	Number Filters
93	Select Specific Data
94	Create a Chart
96	Import a List
97	Create a Table
98	Add Totals to Table
100	Computed Column
102	Table Lookup
104	Manage Data using Access
106	Add Records

Import Data

You don't always need to type in all the information in your worksheets if the data is already available in another application. For example, to import data from a delimited text file:

1 Click the **File** tab and select **Open**

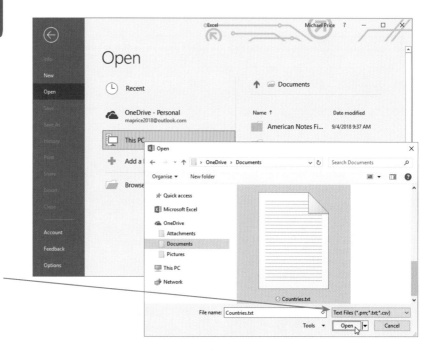

Don't forget

Identify the appropriate file type to select from; in this case, "Text Files".

2 Select the file that contains the data you wish to import and click **Open** to start the Text Import Wizard, which recognizes the delimited file. Click **Next** to continue

Hot tip

Select **My data has headers** if appropriate, so that the header line is treated separately.

3 Check the delimiter type (e.g. **Comma**) and click **Next**

When you choose a delimiter, you can see the effect on the text in the preview area.

4 Adjust column formats, if required, then click **Finish**

The default format is **General**, which will handle most situations, but you can select specific data formats where appropriate.

5 The data is presented in the form of an Excel worksheet

Excel can retrieve data from any application that can create files in a delimited text file format, such as CSV (comma-separated values), or from database systems such as SQL Server, Access, dBase, FoxPro, Oracle, and Paradox.

Explore the Data

1 Double-click or drag the separators between the columns to reveal more of the data they contain

Select the **File** tab, click **Save As** and choose file type Excel Workbook, to save the data as a standard Excel file.

2 Select the **View** tab, click **Freeze Panes** in the Window group, and select **Freeze Top Row**

Hot tip

Freezing the top row makes the headings it contains visible, whichever part of the worksheet is being displayed.

3 Press **Ctrl** + **End** to move to the last row in the data area, and the last occupied cell in that row

Hot tip

This will show you how many rows and columns there are in the data (in this example, 253 rows and 6 columns).

Note that the initial row with the header information is still displayed, even when you view the end of the data area.

Sort

1 Click a cell in the "Country Code" column, select the **Data** tab and click **A-Z** to sort alphabetically, ascending

You can also select the **Sort** options from within the Editing group on the **Home** tab.

2 Click a cell in the "Population" column and click the **Z-A** button to sort numerically, descending (highest to lowest)

Hot tip

If you click in a single cell, Excel will select all the surrounding data and sort the rows of contiguous data into the required order.

3 To sort by more than one value, first click the **Sort** button to launch the Sort dialog box

You can sort the data into sequence using several levels of values.

…cont'd

4 Click the arrow in the **Sort by** box and select the main sort value; for example, "Region"

If a selection of the worksheet is highlighted when you click one of the buttons, the sort may be restricted to the selected data.

5 Click the **Add Level** button and select the additional sort values; for example, "Population"

6 Change the sort sequence, if needed, then click **OK** to sort the data here by "Region" and by "Population"

Don't forget

For data organized by columns, rather than rows, click the **Options...** button and select **Sort left to right**.

	A	B		C	D	E	F
1	Country Code	Name		Region	Capital	Population	Area
166	GI	Gibraltar		Europe		27884	6.5
167	AX	Aland		Europe		26711	1580
168	SJ	Svalbard and Jan Mayen		Europe		2550	62049
169	VA	Vatican City		Europe		921	0.4
170	US	United States		North America		310232863	9629091
171	MX	Mexico		North America		112468855	1972550
172	CA	Canada		North America		33679000	9984670
173	GT	Guatemala		North America		13550440	108890
174	CU	Cuba		North America		11423000	110860
175	DO	Dominican Republic		North America		9823821	48730
176	HT	Haiti		North America		9648924	27750

Filters

You can filter the data to hide entries that are not of immediate interest.

1 Click a cell within the data area, select the **Data** tab and click the **Filter** button in the Sort & Filter group

Hot tip

You can also select the **Filter** button from within the Editing group on the **Home** tab (see page 89).

2 Click a filter icon (e.g. "Region") to display its **AutoFilter**

3 Uncheck the **(Select All)** box, to deselect all entries, then select the specific entry you want; e.g. check "Oceania"

4 Click **OK** to apply the filter

Hot tip

Filtering is turned on, and a filter icon (an arrow) is added to each heading, with an initial setting of **Showing All**.

Number Filters

1 Display the **AutoFilter** for "Population", and choose all entries **Greater Than Or Equal To...** a value of 100,000

Don't forget

You can set number filters to specify a level at which to accept or reject entries, or choose an option such as accepting the top ten entries.

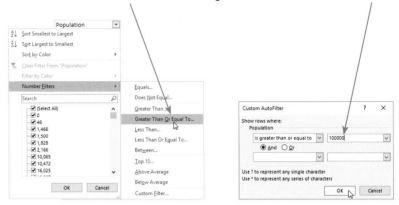

2 The filter button icon is changed, to show that filtering is in effect for the modified **AutoFilter** column

Hot tip

Use **Format Cells** on the **Home** tab to include a comma separator in columns containing numeric data.

3 Click a filter icon and select the **Clear Filter** option to remove the filter for a particular column

Beware

If you click the **Filter** button on the **Data** tab, or the **Home** tab, it will remove all the filters and delete all filter settings.

4 The filter icon for that column reverts to an arrow, and the **Showing All** option will be applied

Select Specific Data

Suppose you want to select only countries with a large population; you can hide away information that's not relevant for that purpose:

1 Use the **AutoFilter** on the "Population" column to display only countries whose population **is greater than** a value of 150 million

2 Select all irrelevant columns. For example, hold down **Ctrl** and click columns: A ("Country Code"), C ("Region"), D ("Capital"), and F ("Area")

3 Now, select the **Home** tab and click **Format, Hide & Unhide, Hide Columns**

4 You will now display only relevant data

Hot tip

Filter the rows and hide selected columns to remove the data not needed at the moment from view.

Don't forget

This places the column of country "Name" adjacent to the column of "Population", ready for further analysis – creating a chart, for example. To help with this, you might sort the information; e.g. in descending numeric order of "Population".

Create a Chart

 Highlight the data (including headers), then select the **Insert** tab and click the Charts group arrow button

Hot tip

Explore each category of chart type to discover numerous sub-type options.

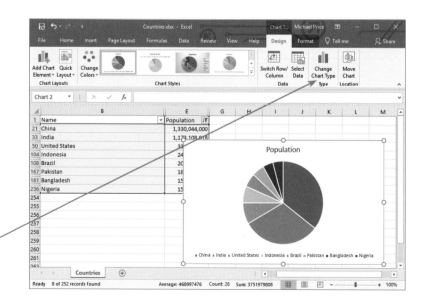 Choose the chart type you require; in this case, a **Pie** chart

Hot tip

When you've created a chart, the **Chart Tools Design** and **Format** tabs are displayed, where you can select other chart styles or use the **Change Chart Type** button to try one of the other chart options.

3 For your chart style, right-click on the population data segments and select **Add Data Labels**

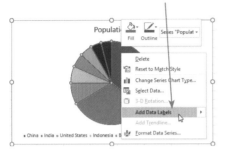

4 Right-click a data label, select **Format Data Labels**, adjust the **Label Position**, and add **Legend key** and adjust its position

5 Click a component, then click it again to edit it. For example, edit the "Population" title component's text content

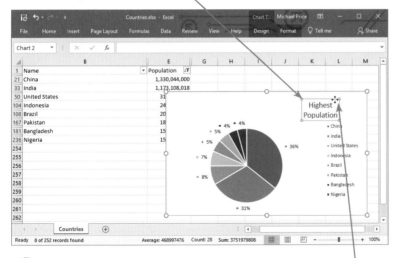

6 Click a component, then move the cursor to its bounding box to reveal the drag handle, to drag and reposition the component in the chart

Import a List

The "Countries" worksheet includes an empty "Capital" column. This data is listed in a text file of "Country" codes and their "Capital" cities, which can be imported into the worksheet.

In the sample worksheet, the original "Capital" column has no data, but this information is available in a separate data file.

Code	Name	Region	Capital	Population	Area
AF	Afghanistan	Asia		29121286	647500
AX	Aland	Europe		26711	1580
AL	Albania	Europe		2986952	28748
DZ	Algeria	Africa		34586184	2381740

 Select a cell marking the start of an empty section of the worksheet, and then click the **Data** tab

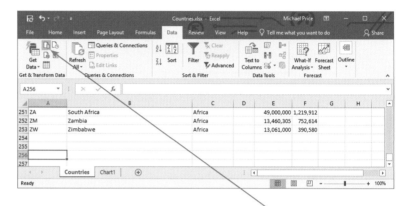

 In **Get & Transform Data** click on **From Text/CSV**

Locate the text file and click **Import**, to get the data

Deliminator and data types are detected. To make adjustments click **Edit**

The contents of the text file are analyzed and the data types and the deliminator are automatically detected.

Select **Use First Row as Headers** then select **Close & Load To...**

Create a Table

1 Choose to view the imported data as a table, select **Existing worksheet** as the location for the data and click **OK**

2 The table will be created using the default style

Don't forget

When you create a table from a data range, any connection with the external data source will be removed.

Hot tip

In previous releases, data would be installed as a named range and you would be required to convert this into a table.

3 Click the **Design** tab and select **Quick Styles** to choose your preferred style for the table

Hot tip

The default name for the table is selected from the imported file (in this case "Capitals") but you can change this if you wish.

Table Name:
Capitals
🔲 Resize Table
Properties

Add Totals to Table

1 Click a cell within the original country data and select **Insert**, **Table**, then rename the new table as "Countries"

Hot tip

Convert the range of country data into table form, then add totals.

2 Select the **Table Tools**, **Design** tab, then check the box for the **Total Row**, to add that row at the end of the table

Don't forget

The functions that you choose are entered into the formula as numbered sub-functions of the **Subtotal** function:
101 (Average)
102 (Count numbers)
103 (Count)
104 (Max)
105 (Min)
107 (StdDev)
109 (Sum)
110 (Variance)

3 Select the "Name" column cell on the **Total Row**, click its arrow button and choose an appropriate function to apply to that column; for example, choose **Count**

4 See the total count of country names appear, then select the **Sum** function for a column with numerical values, such as the "Population" column to see total population

Country Code	Name	Region	Capital	Population	Area	G	H	I	J
253 ZW	Zimbabwe	Africa		13,061,000	390580				
254 Total		252		6,876,071,243					

E254 • fx =SUBTOTAL(109,[Population])

Hot tip

Do not use the column and row labels to specify cells and ranges. Instead, use the table header name for the column (enclosed in square brackets).

5 You can use functions such as **Max** (sub-function 104) and **Min** (sub-function 105) to show the range of values in a column; e.g. to display the largest country "Area"

F254 • fx =CONCATENATE("Largest is ",SUBTOTAL(104,[Area]))

Country Code	Name	Region	Capital	Population	Area	G	H	I	J
253 ZW	Zimbabwe	Africa		13,061,000	390580				
254 Total		252		6,876,071,243	Largest is 17100000				

Don't forget

You can use any Excel function in the total boxes, not just sub-functions of the **Subtotal** function.

99

6 When a column contains a set of discrete values, such as "Region", you can compute the number of unique values it contains; e.g. to display the unique number of "Region". Concatenate a descriptive label if desired

C254 • fx {=SUM(1/COUNTIF([Region],[Region]))}

Country Code	Name	Region	Capital	Population	Area	G	H	I	J
253 ZW	Zimbabwe	Africa		13,061,000	390580				
254 Total		252	8	6,876,071,243	Largest is 17100000				

This is an array formula that counts the number of times each particular value in the column is repeated, and uses these repeats to build up a count of the number of distinct values.

Hot tip

Type an array formula without the enclosing { } curly braces, then press **Ctrl + Shift + Enter** (instead of the usual **Enter**) and the braces are added automatically.

Computed Column

You can add a column to the table without affecting other ranges, data, or tables in the worksheet.

1 Click in the "Area" column, select the **Home** tab, click **Insert**, and choose **Insert Table Columns to the Right**

Hot tip

If you select a cell in the last column of the table, you can insert a column to the left or the right; otherwise, you can only insert a column to the left of the selected cell.

2 The new column is inserted, and it is initially named "Column1"

3 Select the new column header, type a new name, such as "Density", and press **Enter**

Don't forget

The column names are used in the formulas, so it is best to choose meaningful names.

This column can now be used to show population density.

1 Click in the first cell of the "Density" column and type =, then click the "Population" column cell in the same row

The cell that you select is referenced as the current row of the "Population" column, in the formula as: **[@Population]**.

2 Type /, then click the "Area" column cell in the same row

The next cell you select is referenced as: **[@Area]**.

3 Press **Enter**. The expression is evaluated and copied to all the other cells in the table's "Density" column, showing the population density for each country in the list

Country Code	Name	Region	Capital	Population	Area	Density
AD	Andorra	Europe		84,000	468	179.49
AE	United Arab Emirates	Asia		4,975,593	82880	60.03
AF	Afghanistan	Asia		29,121,286	647500	44.97
AG	Antigua and Barbuda	North America		86,754	443	195.83
AI	Anguilla	North America		13,254	102	129.94
AL	Albania	Europe		2,986,952	28748	103.90
AM	Armenia	Asia		2,968,000	29800	99.60
AN	Netherlands Antilles	North America		300,000	960	312.50
AO	Angola	Africa		13,068,161	1246700	10.48
AQ	Antarctica	Antarctica		0	14000000	0.00
AR	Argentina	South America		41,343,201	2766890	14.94
AS	American Samoa	Oceania		57,881	199	290.86
AT	Austria	Europe		8,205,000	83858	97.84
AU	Australia	Oceania		21,515,754	7686850	2.80
AW	Aruba	North America		71,566	193	370.81
AX	Aland	Europe		26,711	1580	16.91
AZ	Azerbaijan	Asia		8,303,512	86600	95.88
BA	Bosnia and Herzegovir	Europe		4,590,000	51129	89.77

The result is the population density – the number of people per square kilometer, formatted to two decimal places.

101

Table Lookup

The example "Countries" table contains a column for the name of the capital city of each country, which is presently empty:

The "Capitals" table was created from an imported text list (see pages 96-97).

The capital city names are stored in the separate "Capitals" table, which was imported into the spreadsheet from a text file at an earlier stage:

Hot tip

VLOOKUP is the vertical-lookup function, used to seek values stored in a table column. There is also a **HLOOKUP** horizontal-lookup function you can use to seek values stored in a table row.

An Excel function named **VLOOKUP** (vertical lookup) can be used to populate the empty "Capital" column in the "Countries" table, using the "Capitals" table:

 Click the first cell of the "Capital" column in the "Countries" table and type the expression **=VLOOKUP(**

...cont'd

2 Click the first cell in the "Country Code" column of the "Countries" table, to specify that you want the function to search for country code values – a reference to the "Country Code" column gets added to the formula

3 Complete the formula by specifying the table in which to search (**Capitals**), the column number in that table whose value is sought (**2**), and (**0**) to indicate that you will only accept an exact match

4 Press **Enter** to fill the empty column with the correct capital name that is associated with each country code

Manage Data using Access

If you have large amounts of data, or complex functions to carry out, you may require the more comprehensive data management facilities that are in Access.

To illustrate the use of Access:

1 Select **Access** from the Start menu or the Taskbar, and you'll be greeted by a range of database template tiles

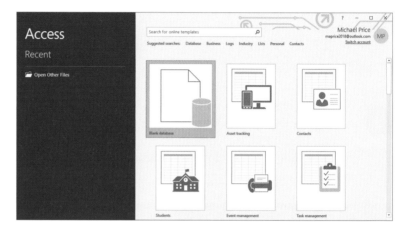

2 Select a category, such as **Personal**, to display a list of the related templates that are available for download from internet sources

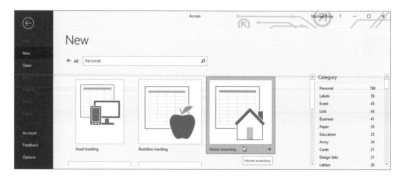

3 Select any template tile to view a description of what that template can be used for, and to download it to your system if it is something you might wish to use

Hot tip

You'll find Access 2019 in Office Professional 2019, and Microsoft 365. It appears only on the Start menu, but you can also pin it to the Taskbar beside your other Office app launcher icons.

4 When you've found the template that you want to use, specify a file name and preferred location on your system, or accept the suggested defaults

The template will be stored in the Recent templates area and will be immediately available for reuse when you select **File**, **New** to create a database.

5 Click the **Create** button to download that template to your computer

6 Access prepares the template for use as a new database, but the database is opened with active content disabled

Do not enable content in databases that you download from internet websites, unless you are sure that the source of the file is trustworthy.

7 Click **Enable Content** to enable the VBA macros in the template and to prepare the database for updating with related data

Add Records

Click the **New Asset** button to launch the Asset Details dialog, in which you can add a record to the database

You can type directly into the cells of the asset table if you prefer, rather than using the form.

Enter the details for the item, selecting values from the list for fields with a drop-down arrow; e.g. **Category**

You can attach links to associated documents, or photos of the asset if you wish, as seen here.

Click **Save and New**, to save the current record and then begin a new record, or click **Close** to return to the list

The current record is automatically saved when you click **Close**, even if all the details are not completed.

6 Presentations

Build a presentation, slide by slide, apply themes to create a consistent effect, and use animation to focus attention on particular points. Use a second monitor for a presenter view, and take advantage of templates – built-in or downloaded – and print handouts for the presentation. Rehearse the show to get timings, and create an automatic show.

108 Start a Presentation

110 Expand the Slide

111 Insert a Picture

112 Apply a Theme

114 Animations

115 Run the Show

116 Other Views

118 Presenter View

120 Choose a Template

122 Use the Template

123 Print the Slide Show

124 Rehearse Timings

125 Save As Options

126 Package for CD

Start a Presentation

To start PowerPoint and create a presentation:

 Launch the PowerPoint application, using any of the methods described on pages 12 and 13 – via the Start menu, Taskbar icon or Search box; or ask Cortana

Hot tip

When PowerPoint opens, it presents a single, blank title slide, ready for you to begin a new presentation.

 Click **Blank Presentation** to open a new presentation at the first slide – to add slide show titles

 Now, select **Click to add title**, then type the title for your slide show; for example, "Origami"

Don't forget

By default, the presentation starts with a title slide, where two text boxes are predefined. If you don't want a particular text box, just ignore it – it won't appear on the slide unless you edit the text.

 Next, select **Click to add subtitle**, and type in the subtitle for your slide show, for example, "The Japanese Art Of Paper Folding"

Select the **Home** tab and click the **New Slide** button in the Slides group

Choose **Title and Content** to add a new slide that provides text boxes for a title and content

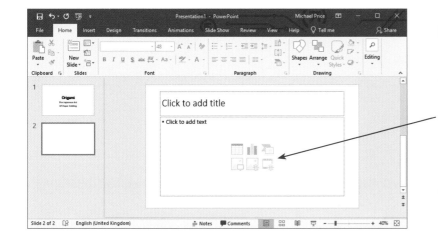

Hot tip

The new **Title and Content** slide has option buttons to **Insert Table**, **Insert Chart**, **Insert a SmartArt Graphic**, **Pictures**, **Online Pictures**, or **Insert Video**. See page 111 for an example.

Click on the prompts and add the title "The History of Origami", then type bullet points to give the details

Don't forget

Click within a bullet item and press **Alt + Shift + Right Arrow** to promote it (move up) to the next higher level.

- Level One
  - Level Two
    - Level Three
      - Level Four

Press **Alt + Shift + Left Arrow** to demote it (move down) to the next lower level.

 Press **Enter** to add a new bullet item, and then press the **Tab** key to move to the next lower level of bullet items

Expand the Slide

 Click the button to save your presentation

2 Continue to add items and you'll see the text size and spacing adjusts to fit the text onto the slide

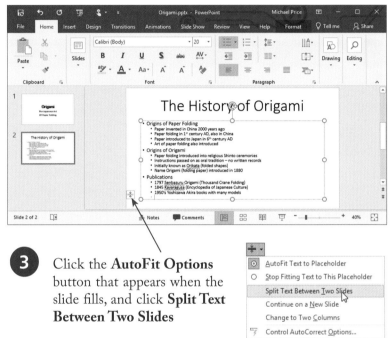

Don't forget

Alternatively, you can choose options to **Stop Fitting Text to This Placeholder**, to **Continue on a New Slide,** or **Change to Two Columns** layout.

3 Click the **AutoFit Options** button that appears when the slide fills, and click **Split Text Between Two Slides**

○ AutoFit Text to Placeholder
○ Stop Fitting Text to This Placeholder
Split Text Between Two Slides
Continue on a New Slide
Change to Two Columns
Control AutoCorrect Options...

4 A new slide is inserted, with the same layout and title, and the bulleted items shared between the two slides

Hot tip

The text size and spacing will be readjusted to take advantage of the extra space available.

Insert a Picture

 Select the **Home** tab, then click the
arrow on the **New Slide** button in the
Slides group to display the options

 Choose a slide layout, such as **Picture
with Caption**

 Now, select **Click icon to add picture**

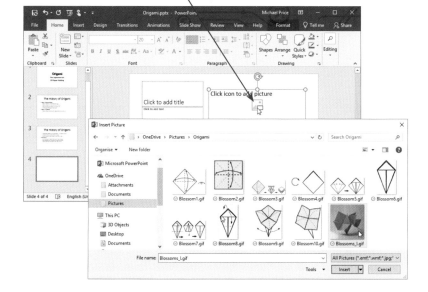

There are nine standard
layouts for slides, so you
can select the one that's
most appropriate for the
specific content planned
for each slide.

The title and the text you
add provide the caption
for the inserted image.

4 Locate and select the image file and click **Insert**, then
select in turn **Click to add title**, and **Click to add text**

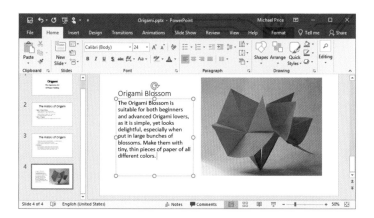

Insert the other slides
needed to complete your
presentation.

111

Apply a Theme

The default slides have a plain background, but you can choose a more attractive theme and apply it to all the slides you've created.

 Select the **Design** tab, then move the mouse pointer over each of the themes to see the effect

 You can scroll the list to display additional themes, change the colors, fonts, and effects for the current theme, and modify the type of background style it uses

Apply to All Slides
Apply to Selected Slides
Delete...
Set as Default Theme
Add Gallery to Quick Access Toolbar

 When you find a theme that you like, click your preferred theme and it will be applied to all of the slides in your presentation

To select the transition effects between slides:

1 Select the **Transitions** tab, then click the **Transition to This Slide** Down arrow to view all of the effects that are available for use

2 Select any effect, then click the **Preview** button to see how it looks and assign it to the current slide

3 Click **None** after running a preview if you decide after viewing it that you don't actually want to assign that effect to the slide

By default, each slide advances to the next slide when you press the mouse key, but you can adjust the setting for individual slides.

1 Uncheck the **Advance Slide, On Mouse Click** box to disable the mouse key for the current slide

2 Check the **After** box and specify a delay time

3 Click the **Apply To All** button to apply the settings to all the slides in the presentation

Whatever the setting, you can always advance the slide show by pressing one of the keyboard shortcuts, such as **N** (next), **Enter**, **Page Down**, **Right Arrow**, or **Spacebar**.

Animations

You can apply animation effects to individual parts of a slide.

 1 Select the **Animations** tab, pick a slide with bullet items, and note that the tab items are grayed out (inactive)

 2 Select any object within the current slide you wish to animate, to see the **Animations** tab items become active

There is a choice of **Entrance**, **Emphasis**, or **Exit** animations, and the **Effect Options** button lets you choose how they should be applied.

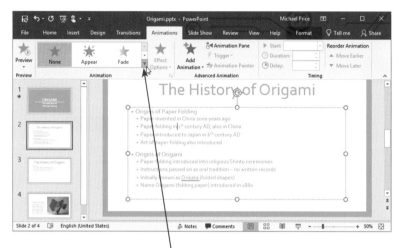

3 Click the Down arrow on the Animation group selection box, then choose an animation to see how it looks and assign it to the current slide. For example, choose **Fly In**

Select **Add Animation** in the Advanced Animation group, if you want to apply additional effects to the slide.

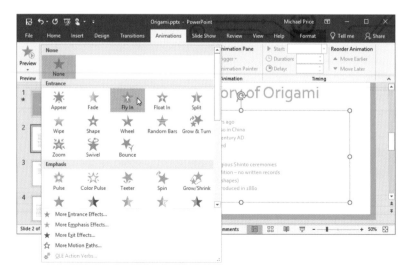

Run the Show

When you've added all the slides you need, you can try running the complete show, to see the overall effect.

1 Select the **Slide Show** tab and click the **From Beginning** button in the Start Slide Show group

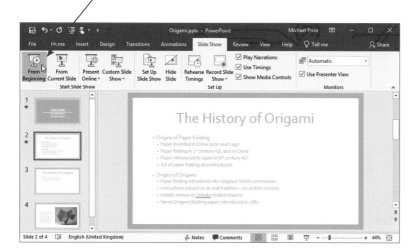

2 The slides are displayed full-screen, with the transition and animation effects that you selected

The History of Origami

- Origins of Paper Folding
  - Paper invented in China 2000 years ago
  - Paper folding in 1st century AD, also in China
  - Paper introduced to Japan in 6th century AD
  - Art of paper folding also introduced

- Origins of Origami
  - Paper folding introduced into religious Shinto ceremonies
  - Instructions passed on as oral tradition – no written records
  - Initially known as Orikata (folded shapes)
  - Name Origami (folding paper) introduced in 1880

3 Click the mouse or keyboard shortcut to advance the slide show, animation by animation, or wait the specified time

4 Review each slide in turn through to the end of the show

Hot tip

You can also press **F5** to run the slide show from the beginning, press **Shift** + **F5** to run from the current slide, or press **Esc** to terminate.

Don't forget

You'll see your selected transition effects and selected animations; in this case, **Fly In** text from the bottom of the slide.

Hot tip

When the slide show finishes, a black screen is presented, with the message: **End of slide show, click to exit**.

End of slide show, click to exit.

Other Views

1 Select the **View** tab and select **Slide Sorter** to display all the slides, so that you can rearrange their sequence

This view is helpful when you have a large number of slides, since you can simply drag slides into their new positions.

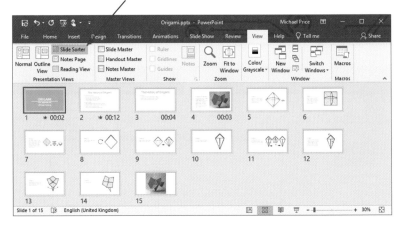

There's also a **Reading View** button, provided in the Presentation Views group on the **View** tab, which allows you to view the slide show in an easily readable format.

2 Select the **Notes Page** view to see the current slide with its notes (information and prompts for the presenter)

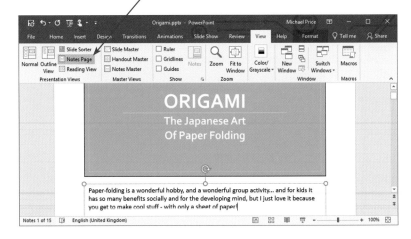

In Notes Page view, each slide and its notes will be displayed on a single sheet, which can be printed to make a very useful handout.

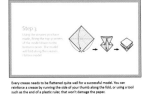

3 Click the 🔍 **Zoom** button, or drag the slider on the Zoom bar, to examine the slide or notes in detail

4 Click the 🔳 **Fit to Window** button, or select **Fit** and click **OK** on the Zoom menu, to resize the view and make the whole page visible

5 To switch back to the view with slide bar and current slide, click the **Normal** button

The view you select will be retained when you select another tab, so you should revert to the required view before leaving.

6 To reveal more of the notes area, click the **Notes** button on the status bar, then drag the separator bar upwards

7 Click the **Outline View** button to see the text content of the slides given in a summary view of the presentation

The buttons to the left of the Zoom bar are another way to select **Normal**, **Slide Sorter**, **Reading View**, and **Slide Show** views.

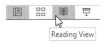

8 Scroll the summary area as needed to view all the slides

Presenter View

 1 Select the **Slide Show** tab, and check the box to enable the **Use Presenter View** option

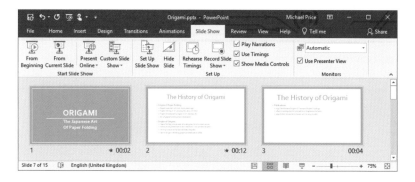

2 If you have a second monitor attached, right-click the Desktop and select **Display settings**

3 **Settings** opens at **Display** showing the monitors that are connected

4 Scroll to **Multiple displays** and select **Extend these displays**

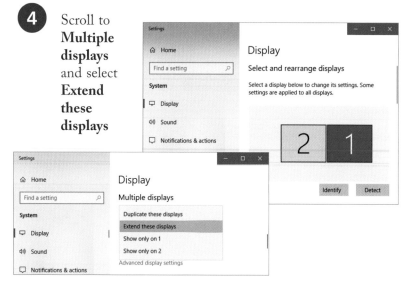

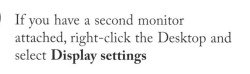
5 Click **Apply**, then click **Keep Changes** when prompted and click **OK** to enable multiple display output for your presentation

6 Select the **Slide Show** tab and click **From Beginning** to run the slide show on the two monitors

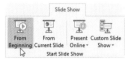

The first monitor gives the presenter's view, with the current slide and its associated notes, plus a preview of the next slide. There's also a Slide bar, to change the sequence of slides during the show.

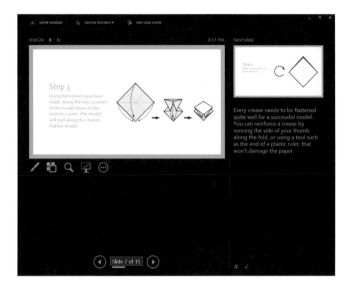

If you do not have a second monitor or projector attached, you can still select **Presenter View** and press **Alt + F5** to run the show from the presenter's view only.

The second monitor is for your audience and displays the current slides in full-screen mode, and changing in full sync with the presenter's monitor.

Use the **Zoom** button to enlarge the notes and make them easier to read while giving the presentation.

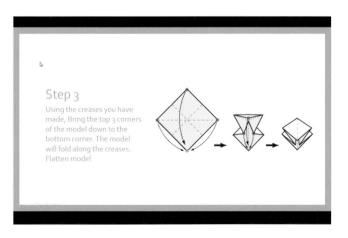

Choose a Template

 In PowerPoint, select the **File** tab, then click **New** to display the example templates provided

Hot tip

Templates provide ready-built presentations, which can be adapted to your needs. They also offer examples of useful PowerPoint techniques.

 Select a template (for example, **Slice**) to see details and view images using the themes and colors offered

Don't forget

You can also enter your own keywords if you want to make a more specific search for suitable templates.

 To make a presentation using the template, click **Create**; otherwise, close the overview and review other templates

 You can use one of the suggested categories (for example, **Business**) to search for online templates and themes

5 PowerPoint searches online for relevant templates and themes of your selected category

6 Thumbnails and links are displayed for the items located, and the associated sub-categories are also listed

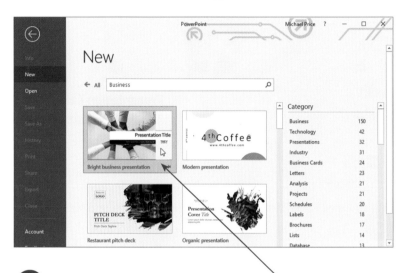

PowerPoint shows the number of templates in each sub-category, and you can select these to identify more closely a suitable template.

7 Select, for example, the **Bright business presentation**, and you'll see it consists of 11 slides with comprehensive help and guidance for creating effective business presentations

8 Click **Create** and the template will be downloaded

The templates that you download and review will be added to the templates displayed when you select **File**, **New** in future sessions.

9 A presentation based upon the template will be opened

Use the Template

 1 When you create a new presentation with a template, it opens showing the predefined slides and content

You can revise the text, add and replace images with your own pictures, and make your own presentation based on the template.

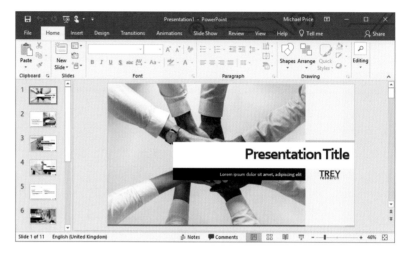

 2 You can edit any of the slides, remove unnecessary slides or add new slides (using the same theme if desired)

 3 To make it easier to reorder the slides, select the **View** tab and click **Slide Sorter**

The template will be retained in its original form in case you want to use it again in the future.

4 Save the presentation with a new name, to preserve the changes

Print the Slide Show

1 Select the **File** tab, then click the **Print** button to specify the printer and other printing options

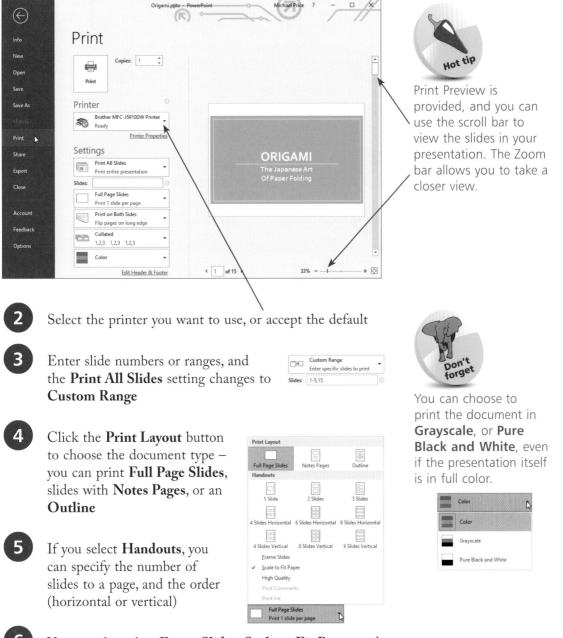

Print Preview is provided, and you can use the scroll bar to view the slides in your presentation. The Zoom bar allows you to take a closer view.

2 Select the printer you want to use, or accept the default

3 Enter slide numbers or ranges, and the **Print All Slides** setting changes to **Custom Range**

You can choose to print the document in **Grayscale**, or **Pure Black and White**, even if the presentation itself is in full color.

4 Click the **Print Layout** button to choose the document type – you can print **Full Page Slides**, slides with **Notes Pages**, or an **Outline**

5 If you select **Handouts**, you can specify the number of slides to a page, and the order (horizontal or vertical)

6 You can also select **Frame Slides**, **Scale to Fit Paper**, and **High Quality** printing

Rehearse Timings

To establish the timings for each slide, you may need to rehearse the presentation and record the times for each step.

You can make the presentation easier to run by assigning timings to the slides, so that it can run automatically.

 Select the **Slide Show** tab and click the **Rehearse Timings** button in the Set Up group

 The slide show runs full-screen in manual mode, with the timer superimposed in the top-left corner

The timer shows the duration so far for the individual slide, and for the presentation as a whole.

 Advance each slide or animation, allowing for viewing and narration, and the times will be recorded

 When the presentation finishes, you can choose to keep the new slide timings for the next time you view the show

Microsoft PowerPoint ✕

The total time for your slide show was 0:00:44. Do you want to save the new slide timings?

Yes   No

Select the **Transitions** tab to make further adjustments to the times for particular slides.

⑤ The view changes to **Slide Sorter,** with individual times for the slides. Make sure that **Use Timings** is selected

Save As Options

1 Select the **File** tab and the Info view is selected, with all the details of the presentation file

There are several formats you can save your PowerPoint Presentation in, enabling you to share it with other users.

2 Click **Save As**, choose a location, then click the **Save as type** box, to see which file formats are supported

3 The PowerPoint Presentation (**.pptx**) format is the default, and is the file type that is designed for editing the presentation

4 Select one of the PowerPoint Show formats (**.ppsx or .ppsm**) format for a file type that is protected from modification. This will open in the **Slide Show** view

Save in the **PowerPoint 97–2003 Presentation** (**.ppt**) format or **PowerPoint 97–2003 Show** (**.pps**) format, to allow users with older versions of PowerPoint to view (or modify) the presentation.

Package for CD

 With the presentation open, select the **File** tab, **Export**, **Package Presentation for CD** and then **Package for CD**

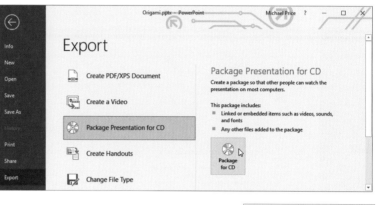

Hot tip

You can also create a PDF or XPS document or create a video of the presentation, to send as email attachments perhaps, or create printed handouts.

 Type a name for the CD, then click **Copy to Folder...**

 Edit the folder name and location, if necessary, then click **OK**

 The presentation files are added to the folder, along with all the files needed to run the PowerPoint Viewer

Don't forget

The package will include any linked or embedded items required, such as videos, sounds and fonts.

 Confirm that you have everything you need, then go back to the Package for CD dialog (see Step 2) and this time select **Copy to CD**. You'll be prompted to insert a blank CD, and the files will be added

7 Office Extras

There are extras included with Microsoft Office, in the form of Office Tools. There are related apps to be found in Microsoft Store as well as tools provided with Windows 10. These include OneNote, which replaces the OneNote product in Office.

128 Office Tools

129 Database Compare

130 Office Language Preferences

132 Spreadsheet Compare

134 Microsoft Store Tools

136 Office Lens

138 Third Party Office Tools

140 Windows 10 Tools

142 OneNote

144 OneNote 2016

Office Tools

The Office suite includes a set of tools as well as applications. You can check which tools have been installed on your system:

 Click **Start** and scroll the **All Apps** list to locate the entry for **Microsoft Office Tools**

 Expand the list to display the tools that are available; in this example, a total of seven items

 Right-click any of the tools and select **More**, **Open file location** to display the folder of shortcuts

 File Explorer opens to show all the shortcuts

Note that there is an additional entry in this example: **Project Server Accounts**. This is only present if you have Microsoft Project (see pages 222-223) installed on your system

Database Compare

This tool provides facilities for comparing the structure of different versions of an Access database.

 Select the **Database Compare** tool from **Microsoft Office Tools** on the **All Apps** list

 Select the Access databases that you wish to compare, and choose which elements to review

3 Click **Compare**, and the database comparison report is generated

Don't forget

You may need to install some development tools such as the Microsoft Report Viewer, before you can work with the Database Compare tool.

Hot tip

The report concentrates on changes to the design of the tables, queries and other components, rather than changes to the data content of the tables. This allows you to view changes made by others if the support of the database is shared.

Database Compare Report

Date: Oct 27, 2018 09:58 AM
User: DESKTOP-4CTPO5S\mapri
File 1: C:\Data\EventDB1.accdb
File 2: C:\Data\EventDB2.accdb

Compare Options

Tables	Yes	Macros	Yes
Queries	Yes	Reports	No
Modules	Yes	Forms	No
Pages	No		

Tables

Table	Item	Old Value	New Value	Change Description
Events	Creation Date	10/27/2018 9:44:40 AM	10/27/2018 9:46:43 AM	Table creation date changed.
Events	Modified Date	10/27/2018 9:44:40 AM	10/27/2018 9:46:43 AM	Table modified date changed.
Filters	Creation Date	10/27/2018 9:44:40 AM	10/27/2018 9:46:44 AM	Table creation date changed.
Filters	Modified Date	10/27/2018 9:44:40 AM	10/27/2018 9:46:44 AM	Table modified date changed.

Queries

Name	Old Value	New Value	Change Description
Current Events	10/27/2018 9:44:41 AM	10/27/2018 9:46:44 AM	Query creation date changed.
Current Events	10/27/2018 9:46:28 AM	10/27/2018 9:47:39 AM	Query modified date changed.

Office Language Preferences

This document includes text in French, which confuses the default English (United States) spell checker.

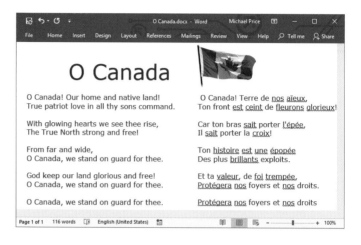

Office supports the use of multiple languages, for the purposes of editing, display, help and screen tips.

You'll have similar problems whenever you need to work with documents that gave text in other languages, or when you use a system with a different language installed; e.g. when traveling.

To check which languages are enabled, and to add a new language:

 Select **Office Languages Preferences** from **Microsoft Office Tools** on the **All Apps** list

 Click the box to **Add additional editing languages** then choose the extra language that you want to add; for example, French (Canada)

You can also open Office Language Preferences in any Office application by selecting the **Review** tab and clicking the **Language** button.

3 Click the **Add** button, then select any other languages you need and repeat the steps to add those as well

You may find it helpful to enable an appropriate keyboard layout for the language you choose.

Editing Language	Keyboard Layout
French (Canada)	Not enabled

Enable a Keyboard Layout in Windows

Enabling a keyboard may make it easier to type text for that language and can help identify the language of the text for spelling and grammar checking. Click "Not enabled" to start enabling a keyboard.

4 Click **OK** and then **OK** again, to apply the changes, then close and restart any Office applications that are open

5 Any test in the new languages will normally be detected, and the appropriate spell checker will be employed

If necessary, select any portion of the text not properly detected; click **Review**, **Language**, **Set Proofing Language...**; and make the proper choice.

Spreadsheet Compare

The Spreadsheet Compare tool lets you pick any two workbooks and compare them very quickly. The differences between the spreadsheets are categorized so you can focus on important aspects, such as changes to formulae.

To see the tool in action:

 Select **Spreadsheet Compare** from **Microsoft Office Tools** on the **All Apps** list

2 Click the **Compare Files** button

3 Select the **Browse** buttons in turn to locate the two spreadsheets that you'd like to compare, then click **OK**

4 The two workbooks are opened and compared, and the results are displayed side by side

In this example it's only data values (populations, ranks and some country names) that are flagged as different.

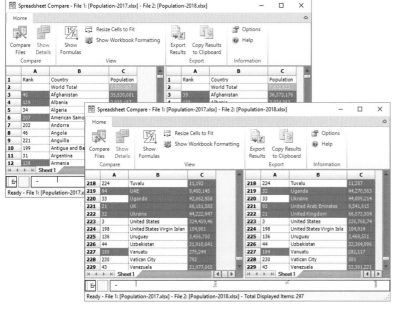

5 Spreadsheet Compare identifies quite complex changes

You can choose to display the formulas in each cell rather than the values, to help identify possible causes for changes.

Here the tax rate has changed, and an extra line has been entered. The tool understands that some items get displaced, and only flags actual differences; e.g. in the tax and the totals.

133

Microsoft Store Tools

A good selection of tools that can be used with Office can be found in the Microsoft Store. To explore what's available:

 Click the icon on the Taskbar to open the Microsoft Store

 Click in the **Search** box, then type "Microsoft To-Do" to locate the associated app

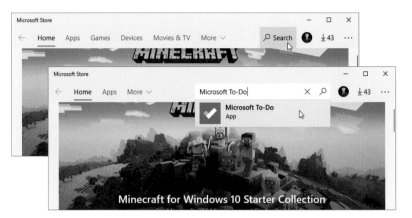

 Select the app in the search results to review its details

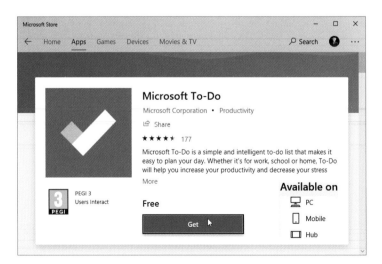

 Click the **Get** button to download and install the app

Microsoft To-Do makes it easy to plan your day, for work, school or home. It includes customizable themes, notes, reminders, due dates, smart suggestions, and syncing across multiple devices. You can use To-Do as a note-taking app, and it works with your Outlook Tasks, making it easier to manage all your tasks in one place. Whether you're at home with your PC, or traveling with your mobile phone or iPad, your tasks and lists will always be available to you.

1 To get started, click the **Microsoft To-Do** in the **All Apps** list

After you have installed Microsoft To-Do, you can also start the app by clicking **Launch** from the app's entry in Microsoft Store.

2 Select **My Day** and click **Add a task** to begin defining your activities

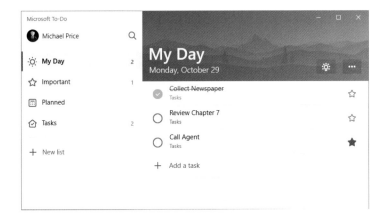

Click on a white star to make a task as important. Click again to remove importance.

3 Click the circle next to a task to toggle between complete and incomplete

Office Lens

Microsoft Store offers another useful app from Microsoft, called Office Lens. Office Lens trims and enhances pictures of whiteboards and docs, and makes them readable. You can use Office Lens to convert images to PDF, Word and PowerPoint files, and you can even save images to OneNote or OneDrive.

It turns your USB camera into a portable scanner in your pocket. It will allow you to digitize notes from presentations, and you can keep copies of important documents or business cards or your receipts. Printed and handwritten text will be automatically recognized (using OCR), so you can search for words in images and then copy and edit them.

To find and install Office Lens:

Hot tip

Office Lens is another app from Microsoft Corporation that again is free of charge.

 Search in Microsoft Store for the app title "Office Lens"

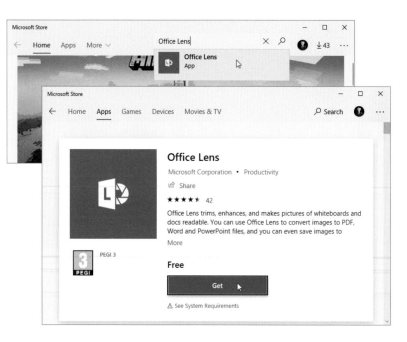

Don't forget

You need a USB digital camera on your system to make use of Office Lens. You also need the camera capabilities of your mobile phone camera with the mobile version of the app.

 Click **Get** to download and install the Office Lens app

3 Click the **Office Lens** entry in the **All Apps** list to launch the app

4 View a document on the desk using the camera, and see how it appears as a skewed image

Don't forget

You can imagine taking snapshots of documents and screen or blackboard presentations like this, and having them improved in this manner.

5 Click the button to snapshot the document, and it is automatically squared up and with background cleared

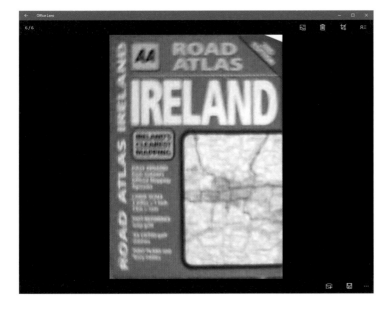

Hot tip

Text and images copied in this fashion can be saved as PDF, Word or PowerPoint files. You can also import existing .JPG, .BMP or .PNG files and process them in this way.

Third Party Office Tools

 1 Search for apps using the term "Office Tools"

To get some idea of the apps available from other suppliers, carry out a more general search in Microsoft Store.

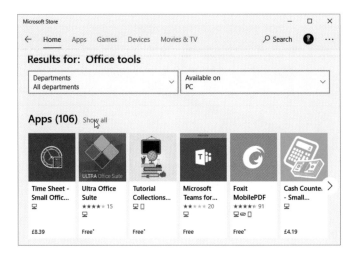

2 This finds more than a hundred apps, mainly from third-party suppliers, with well over half of the apps being free of charge

3 You can also search by category; for example, free apps for **Business, Legal & HR**

There are 25 different categories to choose from, each with a number of subcategories.

 4 Select the Legal Forms and Agreements app to review its details

…cont'd

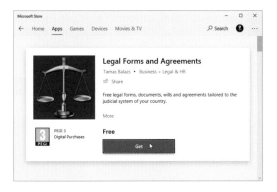

1 Download and install the app, then launch it using the **All Apps** list

2 Select one of the countries then choose a document

3 Follow the prompts to create your version

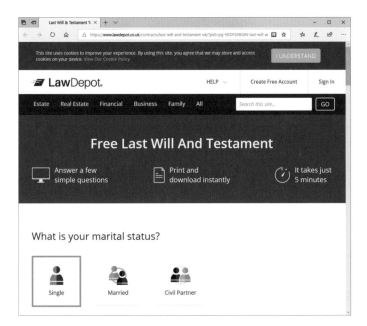

Hot tip

This app contains a variety of documents that meet the legal requirements for the four specified countries.

Australia
Canada
United Kingdom
United States

Hot tip

There are more than 350 different legal forms and agreements in total for the four countries, with instructions and guidance for completing each of them.

Indemnity Agreement
Independent Contractor Agreement
Joint Venture Agreement
Last Will and Testament
Lasting Power of Attorney Registration
Lease Amendment
Lease Assignment Agreement
Letter of Intent
Living Will

Windows 10 Tools

The Windows Calculator app supports a range of computational facilities, and can be a convenient alternative to the full spreadsheet application. To explore its options:

1 Select **Calculator** from **All Apps**

2 Use **Standard** mode for Add, Subtract, Multiply, Divide, Square Root, Percentage, and Inverse operations, aided by Memory and History features

3 Click the **Navigation** button to explore the other options – **Scientific** mode, for example

Scientific mode offers a variety of exponential, logarithmic, trigonometric and factorial functions in various forms, such as Degrees, Radians, etc.

Don't forget

As well as calculation modes, Calculator also features a wide variety of Converter options.

4 We'll leave **Programmer** mode, with its Hex, Dec, Oct and Bin format for the coders, but we'll select **Date Calculation** mode from the **Navigation** list

Calculator
- Standard
- Scientific
- Programmer
- Date Calculation

Converter
- Currency
- Volume
- Length
- Weight and Mass
- Temperature
- Energy
- Area
- Speed
- Time
- Power
- Data
- Pressure
- Angle

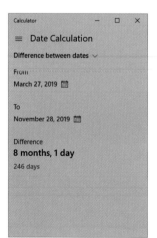

Date Calculation is the simplest mode and has just two functions. It lets you add or subtract days from a date, or it tells you the difference between two dates. However, it is invaluable if you want to know how many days are left until Thanksgiving.

...cont'd

Notepad is a very simple editor that allows you to create, view or modify plain text (.txt) files, with effectively no formatting.

 1 Select **Windows Accessories** from **All Apps**, and within this find the entry for **Notepad**

 2 Type some text, pressing **Enter** for each new line

You can copy the contents of web pages or formatted documents into Notepad, and it will strip off the images and formatting to generate a plain text file.

3 If you find the lines get longer than the window width, select **Format** and then **Word Wrap** so you can see all the text

Select **Edit**, **Go To** and then enter a line number, to go to that line in the file (as shown on the **status bar**).

 4 Type additional text and choose **File**, **Save As...**, to capture your work

5 Pick the folder where you want the file stored, enter the file name and click **OK**

The file is saved to the specified folder, with file type **.txt**, the normal file type for plain text.

Note that **Go To** is disabled and the **status bar** is hidden when you select **Word Wrap**.

OneNote

OneNote for Windows 10, which is known simply as OneNote, is included in all versions of Windows 10 and is also included in Microsoft 365 and Office 2019. OneNote is a digital note-taking app that provides a single place for keeping all of your notes, research, plans, and information. You can capture information in many formats, including web page clips, tables, PowerPoint slides, Outlook meetings, Excel spreadsheets, handwritten notes, and voice recordings.

To begin using OneNote:

 Select **OneNote** from **All Apps**

The first time you launch OneNote it takes a few moments to get things ready for you to use it.

2 When the initial setup completes, click the **Get Started** button

3 OneNote opens with a Notebook, usually called My Notebook, with one section Quick Notes and no pages

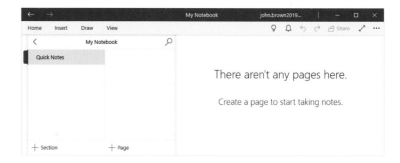

Hot tip

Previous versions of Office had their own version of **OneNote** – **OneNote 2013** in Office 2013 and **OneNote 2016** in Office 2016. Office 2019 does not have its own version, but may sometimes have a copy of **OneNote 2016** (see page 144).

Don't forget

Your Notebook is stored at **OneDrive Online**, with an internet shortcut in your local **OneDrive**.

4 Click **+ Section** to add a new section, and type your preferred name over "New Section 1" as provided

Right-click a section name to see the options available for sections.

5 Add any additional sections desired, then select a section and click **+ Page** to add new pages

Similarly, right-click a page name to see the options for pages.

6 You can type the page title, which becomes the page name. Add any additional pages needed for that section

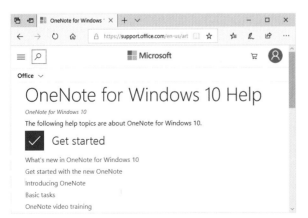

Press **F1** to get online help using the Windows 10 version of **OneNote**.

143

OneNote 2016

If you have upgraded from Office 2016 to Office 2019, you may find that you have two versions of OneNote on your system. You will have OneNote for Windows 10 (see page 142) and OneNote 2016. This product is no longer being developed, but during installation, Office 2019 will detect if you have used OneNote 2016 and if so will make it available.

Microsoft recommends using OneNote for Windows 10, but OneNote 2016 is still optionally available for anyone who needs it – especially if you have locally stored Notebooks previously created. There are also some features that are currently only available in OneNote 2016, including:

- Create Outlook Tasks in your notes.

- Record video.

- Store notebooks on your local hard drive instead of in the Cloud, including backups.

You can even create your Notebook in OneDrive for Windows 10, and access it using OneNote 2016.

To open My Notebook created using OneNote for Windows:

 Select the entry for **OneNote 2016** from the **All Apps** list

 My Notebook opens all the sections and pages previously created, as shown by the Expenses section

The use of OneNote 2016 in this fashion is only recommended if you need some of OneNote 2016's exclusive features.

Don't forget

OneNote for Windows 10 has an increasing number of features that are not available in OneNote 2016; in particular, the ability to share your Notebook on Mac, iOS, Android, and web devices.

Hot tip

You can set the default for opening Notebooks in Windows 10 Settings. Select Apps, Default apps, and choose Set defaults by app.

Choose an app

OneNote

OneNote 2016

Look for an app in the Store

8 Email

The first time you use Outlook, you may need to specify your email account. Then, you can receive messages, save attachments, print messages, issue replies, and update your address book, while also protecting yourself from spam messages that might be targeted at your account. You can add a standard signature note to your messages, and subscribe to RSS feeds.

146   Starting Outlook

148   Your First Messages

149   Turn Off Reading Pane

150   Request a Newsletter

152   Receive a Message

154   Save All Attachments

155   Print the Message

156   Reply to the Message

157   Add Address to Contacts

158   Spam and Phishing

160   Create a Message

161   Insert a Signature

162   Message Tags

163   RSS Feeds

Starting Outlook

The Microsoft Outlook program provides the email and time management functions in Office. To start the application:

1 Select the Outlook tile from the Start menu (or locate the application on the All Apps list or via the Search box)

Microsoft

The fine print

These Microsoft Office Professional Plus 2019 apps are installed:

This product also comes with Office Automatic Updates.
Learn more

By selecting Accept, you agree to the Microsoft Office License Agreement
View Agreement

Accept and start Outlook

The first time you start Outlook, you may be asked to accept the Microsoft Office license agreement. Then, it helps you to define the email accounts you want to manage using this application.

2 Click **Accept and start Outlook** to initiate setup of Outlook with your email account

3 Type the email address you wish to use, and click **Next** to have your account set up automatically

Outlook

maprice19@outlook.com

Advanced options ⌄

Connect

Don't forget

Outlook is found in all editions of Microsoft 365 except for the Home & Student edition.

Outlook will normally detect the requirements for setting up the email account and choose the most effective settings. However, you can select **Advanced options** to allow you to set up the account manually if you find the defaults are unsuitable.

4 The wizard establishes the network connection, and then requests the password for your email account

5 Enter your password and click the box **Remember my credentials**, so you'll connect automatically whenever you start Outlook, then click **OK** to continue

6 The wizard logs on to your account on the server

Hot tip

You could manually configure your account, but the easiest way to add the account is to let the wizard establish the settings for you.

7 Select **Done** to begin using your email account

Your First Messages

Outlook opens with the Inbox, showing your first email messages; e.g. a welcome message from the ISP, or from the Outlook team.

Quick Access Toolbar   Tab bar   Tell Me Help

Ribbon

Collapse/
Expand button

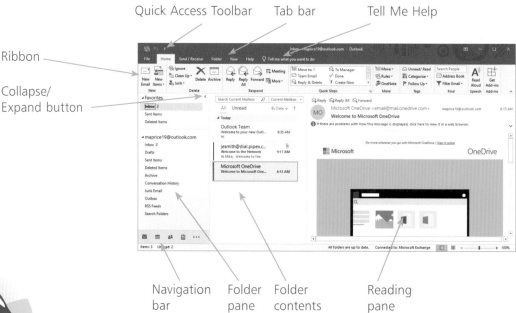

Navigation   Folder   Folder   Reading
bar   pane   contents   pane

Hot tip

Outlook may prevent the automatic download of some pictures in the message. If you trust the source, you can choose to download the pictures.

> ⓘ Click here to download pictures. To help protect your privacy, Outlook prevented automatic download of some pictures in this message.

You can click the **<** button at the top right of the Folder pane to collapse that pane, to provide more space to display more message content, or to cope with a smaller screen size:

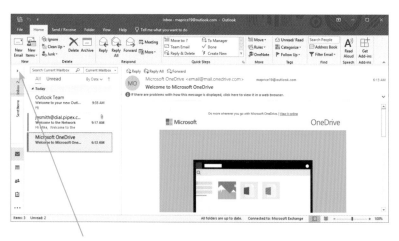

Click the **>** button again to redisplay the Folder pane temporarily. The button changes to a pin. Click this to display the Folder pane on an on-going basis.

Turn Off Reading Pane

1 Select **View**, **Reading Pane**, and reposition **Right** or **Bottom**, or choose **Off**

2 Messages are left unread until opened, and are displayed in lists grouped by date received

 Beware

Simply reading an email message could release harmful software into your system. Turn off the **Reading Pane** and review the message first to avoid potential problems with spam and phishing emails (see pages 158-159).

3 Double-click on any message (or select any message and press **Enter**) to open the message and display its contents

 Don't forget

Unread messages appear in a bold, colored font. Messages that have been opened will appear in a regular font.

4 Select **File** and then **Close** from the action list in the Backstage view to close the message window, or just click the window's [**X**] close button

5 As more messages arrive and time passes, you find them grouped under headings: Today, Yesterday, Previous days this week, Last Week, Last Month or Older

▷ **Today**

▷ **Yesterday**

▷ **Wednesday**

▷ **Last Week**

▷ **Last Month**

▷ **Older**

Request a Newsletter

To begin exchanging messages, you'll need to share your email address with friends, contacts, and organizations.

ITW is an honorary society of authors who write books – fiction and nonfiction – broadly classified as thrillers. The website features a regular newsletter.

In some cases, there may be a fee for the service, though most often the newsletters are provided free of charge, as in this case.

You can also use your email address to request newsletters:

 1 Visit the website **thrillerwriters.org**; a society that offers a free subscription newsletter

2 Scroll down to the link where you apply for a newsletter subscription, and click **Sign up**

3 Enter your **Email Address**, and optionally **First Name** and **Last Name** into the input boxes, then click **Subscribe to list**

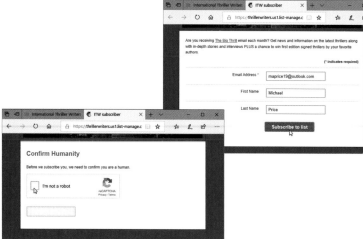

4 Before you can subscribe, you'll be asked to carry out actions to prove you are a person. Begin by clicking the box **I'm not a robot**

5 Carry out the action, in this case selecting squares with traffic lights, and click **Verify** to confirm

6 With your humanity confirmed, you can now click **Subscribe to list** to complete the application

7 Confirmation of your subscription is sent to your Inbox

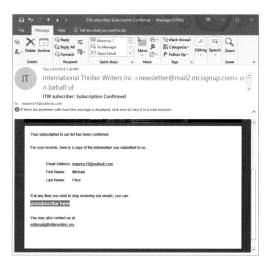

Receive a Message

To check for any mail that may be waiting:

 Open Outlook, select the **Send/Receive** tab, and click **Send/Receive All Folders**

 New mail will be downloaded and displayed in the Inbox

Hot tip

Select the **Send/Receive** tab to get extra functions that give more control over the Send/Receive process.

Don't forget

Depending on the settings, Outlook may automatically issue a Send/Receive when it starts up, and at intervals thereafter. You can also manually check for messages at any time.

 The paperclip icon indicates this message has attachments. Double-click the message title to display the contents

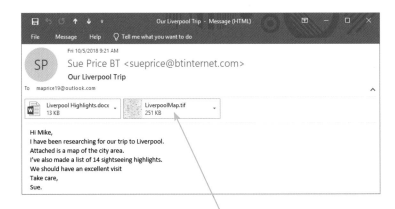

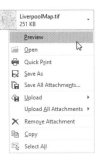

There are icons showing the type, file name and size of each attachment

Click the arrow button next to the icon (or right-click the box) to open a drop-down menu offering choices for dealing with the attachment

6 Click the **Preview** option on the attachment menu to view the attachment within Outlook. Click the **Back to message** button to return to the message

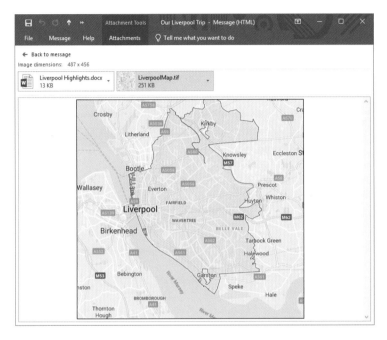

7 Right-click a message for the context menu, offering options such as **Delete** to send it to the Deleted Items folder, or **Move** to a folder that you select

Beware

Email attachments can contain malicious software. Always be suspicious of attachments to messages from unknown sources.

Save All Attachments

To save all the attachments at once:

 Open the message, right-click on any attachment icon and select the **Save All Attachments...** option

2 The list of attachments is displayed, with all the attachments selected

3 Press **Ctrl**, and click any of the attachments to amend the selection, then click **OK** to download the attached files

4 Locate the folder to receive the downloads (or click **New folder** to create a new folder), then click **OK** to save

5 Open the target folder in File Explorer to view the files that you have just saved

Print the Message

1 From the message, select the **File** tab, then click **Print**

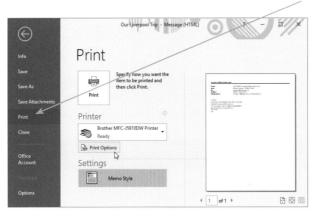

The print preview shows how the message will appear on the page. Select the **Print** button to send the message to the printer, using all the default settings.

2 Click **Print Options** to change the printer or adjust the print settings; e.g. to specify the number of copies you want

3 Check the **Print attached files** box if you also want to print any attachments

4 For picture attachments, you can select the print size for the image; e.g. Full page, or 4 x 6 in.; etc.

Each attachment will print as a separate print job, destined for the default printer. You can change the print size on each job, but you cannot combine the prints onto the same sheet.

Reply to the Message

Hot tip

Click **Reply to All** to reply to multiple addressees, or click **Forward** if you want to share the message with another person.

Beware

The Reading Pane may be active in the Sent folder even if switched off in the Inbox, as it is configured individually for each folder.

Hot tip

Messages to which you have replied are marked with the date and time of your reply.

ℹ You replied to this message on 10/5/2018 2:44 PM.

1 When you want to reply to a message that you've opened, click the **Reply** button in the Respond group on the **Message** tab

2 The message form opens with the email address, the subject entered, and the cursor in the message area, ready for you to type your comments above the original text

To... Sue Price BT <sueprice@btinternet.com>
Cc...
Subject RE: Our Liverpool Trip

Thanks Sue, that's great. I'll add those highlights to our plan.

From: Sue Price BT <sueprice@btinternet.com>
Sent: Friday, October 5, 2018 9:21 AM
To: maprice19@outlook.com
Subject: FwOur Liverpool Trip

Hi Mike,
I have been researching for our trip to Liverpool.

3 Complete typing your response and then click the **Send** button to transfer the response – initially to the Outbox folder, from where a copy will be sent onwards to the destination address

New Email
▷ Favorites
⊿ maprice19@outlook.com
  Inbox 2
  Drafts
  Sent Items
  Deleted Items
  Archive
▷ Conversation History

Search Sent Items — Current Folder
Sent Items — By Date ↑
⊿ Today
'Sue Price BT'   ⚑
RE: Our Liverpool Trip   2:44 PM ✕
Thanks Sue, that's great. I'll add those highlights to our plan. Regards.

Items: 1   All folders are up to date.   Connected to: Microsoft Exchange

4 When the reply has been sent, your copy is moved to the Sent folder to signify completion

Add Address to Contacts

Whenever you receive an email, you can add the email address of the sender (and any other addressees in the message) to your Outlook Contacts list.

1 Right-click the email address and select **Add to Outlook Contacts**

2 Review the data that's pre-entered, and include any extra pieces of information that you may have

3 Click **Save** to record the details in the Contacts list

4 Select the People button to open your Contacts list

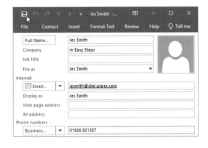

5 Review the new addition to your Contacts list and click the **More (...)** button to select **Edit Outlook Contact** and change entries or add further details as required

Spam and Phishing

As useful as email can be, it does have problem areas. Because it is so cheap and easy to use, the criminally inclined take advantage of email for their own profit. They send out thousands of spam (junk email) messages, in the hope of getting one or two replies.

Beware

Don't respond in any way to messages that you think may be spam. Even clicking on an **Unsubscribe** link will confirm that your address is a genuine email account, and this may get it added to lists of validated account names.

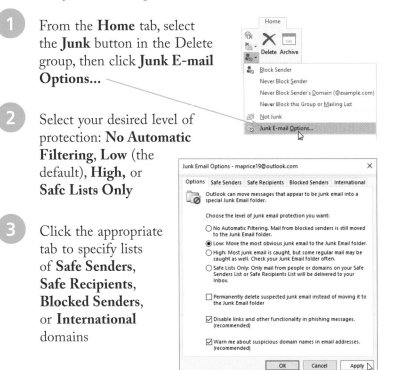

The Outlook Junk Email filter identifies spam as messages are received, and moves the invalid messages to the **Junk Email** folder. To adjust the settings:

Hot tip

Any message sent to the **Junk Email** folder is converted to plain-text format, and all links are disabled. In addition, the **Reply** and **Reply All** functions are disabled.

> ⓘ Links and other functionality have been disabled in this message. To turn on that functionality, move this message to the Inbox. We converted this message into plain text format.

Don't forget

You can block messages from specified top-level domain codes, and messages written in particular foreign languages.

1 From the **Home** tab, select the **Junk** button in the Delete group, then click **Junk E-mail Options...**

2 Select your desired level of protection: **No Automatic Filtering**, **Low** (the default), **High,** or **Safe Lists Only**

3 Click the appropriate tab to specify lists of **Safe Senders**, **Safe Recipients**, **Blocked Senders**, or **International** domains

Outlook also provides protection from messages even when they are allowed into the Inbox:

- Links to pictures on the sender's website may be blocked, links to websites may be disabled, and you may not be allowed to use the **Reply** and **Reply All** functions.

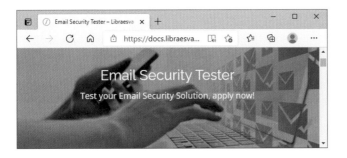

- To explore how Outlook handles potentially damaging messages, visit the website **docs.libraesva.com** and select the **Email Security Tester** link. Submit an email address and respond to the confirming email.

- Review the subsequent emails you receive from this website to see how Outlook responds to the various scenarios. For example, Outlook blocks access to an attachment that's executable and so potentially dangerous.

Links to pictures and other content from a website may be blocked, since these are sometimes the source of viruses and other threats. Only download them if you trust the sender.

Some spam messages and websites try to trick you into providing passwords, PINs, and personal details. Known as phishing (pronounced "fishing"), they appear to be from well-known organizations such as banks, credit card providers, and charities.

The attachments and links in these test emails are innocuous, but do illustrate ways in which the security of your system could be impacted.

Create a Message

Hot tip

You can also select **New Email Message** from the Jump list, which appears when you right-click the program entry on the Taskbar (or right-click the Outlook program entry on the Start menu).

Don't forget

You can send the same message to more than one addressee. You can also select addressees for the **Cc** (courtesy copy) or **Bcc** (blind courtesy copy) options.

Hot tip

The **Attach File** button provides a **Recent Items** list so you can quickly select recent documents to attach to a message.

 Select the **Home** tab and click the **New Email** button to open a mail message form

 Click the **To...** button to open the address book and list your contacts

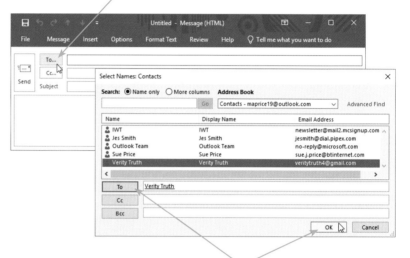

 Select the addressee and click **To**, then add any other addressees and then click **OK**

 Type the subject, greeting, and text for your message

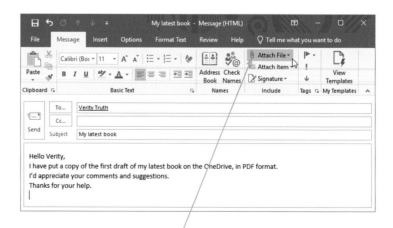

 If required, click **Attach File** and select any files to attach

Insert a Signature

You can create a standard signature to add to the emails you send.

1 Select the **Insert** tab and click **Signature** in the Include group, then click **Signatures...**

2 Click the **New** button to open the New Signature dialog, specify the signature name and click **OK**

3 Add the signature text and click **OK** to save it by name

4 Position the typing cursor where you want to insert a signature, then click **Signature** again and select the name of the signature you want to insert

Hot tip

The first time you select the **Signature** button, there'll be no signatures defined, so you must start off by creating one.

Don't forget

You can specify one of your signatures as the default for new messages, or for replies and forwards, and the appropriate signature will be automatically applied to future messages.

Don't forget

Click the **Send** button to store the message in the Outbox (if you are offline), ready for the next Send. Click the **Send/Receive** tab and select **Send/Receive** to send immediately.

Message Tags

You can use tags to help sort and organize messages.

1 Select a message, then select **Home**

2 Click **Unread/Read** to toggle the read status of the selected message

3 Click **Categorize** to choose a color to associate with the selected message

Beware

Email accounts that use an IMAP connection do not have the **Categorize** tag for their messages.

4 The first time you select a specific color, you'll be asked if you want to rename it, or assign it a shortcut key

162

5 The **CATEGORIES** column is added to the Inbox view, and this can also be used to order the messages

Hot tip

Flagged messages are automatically added to your **Task** list.

6 Click the **Follow Up** button on the Home tab to assign a reminder flag to the selected message

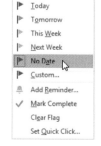

7 Choose when to review the message

RSS Feeds

RSS (Rich Site Summary/Really Simple Syndication) is a way for content publishers to make news, blogs, and other information available to their subscribers, using a standardized XML format that can be viewed by many programs. You can add RSS "feeds" and view subscriptions in the Outlook application.

 1 When you find an RSS feed you would like to subscribe to on a website, you need to copy the feed URL address

You can access and subscribe to RSS feeds in some web browsers. Internet Explorer even has icons to show when RSS feeds are available.

However, the Windows 10 browser Microsoft Edge does not support RSS feeds.

2 Open Outlook, and select the **Folders** view

3 Right-click on the **RSS Feeds** folder, to open its context menu, then choose to **Add a New RSS Feed...**

4 Position the typing cursor in the location box, then press **Ctrl** + **V** to paste in the copied URL, then click **Add**

When you subscribe to an RSS feed it adds its own folder within the **RSS Feeds** folder.

...cont'd

When you subscribe to RSS feeds from a web browser, you can use Outlook to view the updates as they arrive.

5 A dialog asks you to confirm whether you want to add the feed – click the **Advanced...** button

6 Enter an RSS **Feed Name** and select any required configuration changes

7 Click **OK** to close the options panel

8 Now click **Yes** to confirm you want to add the feed, and see the feed items appear in Outlook, in the folder for that feed

To ensure that the feeds remain synchronized, select **File**, **Options**, **Advanced**, and then check the option to **Synchronize RSS Feeds**.

9 Time Management

Outlook is much more than an email manager. It is a complete personal information management system, with full diary and calendar facilities. It enables you to keep track of appointments and meetings, and to control and schedule your tasks. You can keep notes, make journal entries, and correlate all these with email messages relating to those records.

166 Outlook Calendar

167 Schedule an Appointment

168 Change Appointment Details

169 Recurring Appointments

170 Create a Meeting

172 Respond to an Invitation

174 Add Holidays

176 Report Free/Busy Time

177 Schedule a Meeting

178 Creating Tasks

180 Assigning Tasks

181 Accepting Task Requests

182 Confirming the Assignment

184 Outlook Notes

186 Journal

Outlook Calendar

The Outlook Calendar handles time-based activities, including appointments, meetings, holidays, courses, and events (single-day or multi-day). It provides a high-level view by day, week or month and will give you reminders when an activity is due. To open:

1 Click the Calendar button on the Navigation bar

To customize the navigation bar, click the ••• button, then select **Navigation Options...** and choose your preferred options.

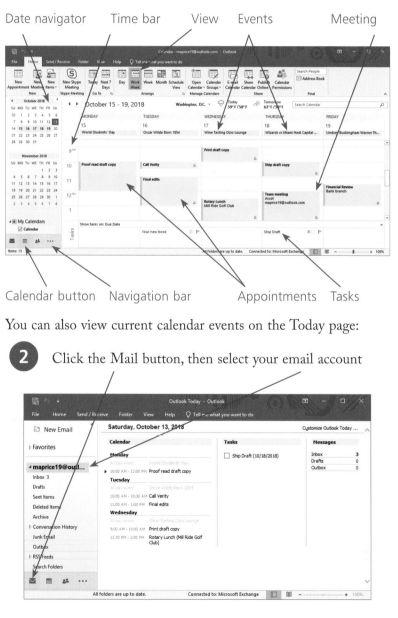

Date navigator   Time bar   View   Events   Meeting

Calendar button   Navigation bar   Appointments   Tasks

You can also view current calendar events on the Today page:

2 Click the Mail button, then select your email account

The Outlook Today page displays a summary of the calendar activities, the tasks, and the counts of unread messages on your system. Click the **Calendar** header to display the full calendar.

Schedule an Appointment

An appointment reserves space in your calendar for an activity that does not involve inviting other people, or reserving resources.

 1 Open the calendar (Day, Week or Month view) and use the date navigator to select the day for the appointment

Hot tip

You can also double-click the Start time area, or right-click that area and select **New Appointment**.

2 Using the mouse pointer select the time the appointment should begin, then click the **New Appointment** button

Don't forget

To change the **End time** and duration, click the Down arrow and select a new value. You can also change the **Start time** (the current duration will be maintained).

3 Type the **Subject**, then select the end time and enter any other details you have, such as **Location** and a description

4 When you've completed the details, press the **Save & Close** button

Change Appointment Details

The appointment is added to the calendar, which shows the subject, start time, duration and location. Move the mouse over the appointment area to see more details.

 Select the appointment, and the **Calendar Tools** tab is added, with related options displayed on the Ribbon

Don't forget

Single-click the calendar at the appointment area and you can edit the text of the subject title. Double-click the area and you will open the appointment for editing.

Hot tip

By default, you will get a reminder pop-up for the appointment 15 minutes before the start time, or you can set your own notice period (values between zero and two weeks), or turn off the reminder completely.

2 Click **Open** (or double-click the appointment) to open the appointment editor form (see page 167), add or change any of the details, and then click **Save & Close**

 Drag the top or bottom edge of the appointment block to change the start or finish times. The duration is adjusted to match the changes

Recurring Appointments

When you have an activity that's repeated on a regular basis, you can define it as a recurring appointment.

 1 Open the appointments form and specify the details for the first occurrence of the activity, then click **Recurrence**

2 Specify frequency and the period of recurrence

3 Click **OK**, then click **Save & Close** to record the changes

4 All of the occurrences of the appointment will be displayed on the appropriate dates in the calendar

You can take an existing appointment or meeting, and click **Recurrence** to make it a recurring activity.

Unless you limit the number of recurrences, or set a termination date, the activity will be scheduled for all possible days in the future.

Depending on the view chosen and the space available, the appointment may be indicated by an icon.

Create a Meeting

1 Double-click the appointment entry in the calendar, and click the **Invite Attendees** button in the Attendees group

Hot tip

You can convert an existing appointment into a meeting by defining the attendees and sending invitations.

2 On the invitation message form displayed, click the **To...** button to open the contacts list

3 Select each attendee and click **Required** or **Optional** for each. When all attendees have been added, click **OK**

Don't forget

You can also schedule meeting resources such as rooms, screens, and projectors.

...cont'd

4 With all the proposed attendees added, you can then click the **Send** button to email the invitation to each of them

You can adjust the Start time, End time, Reminder and other details before you actually send the invitation.

5 The appointment now appears as a meeting in the organizer's calendar

6 Open the meeting to see the current status, which initially shows no responses have been received

Double-click the meeting entry in your calendar, or select the entry and click Open from the Meeting tab, to display the details and the status.

Respond to an Invitation

The attendees need not be using a version of Outlook in order to receive and respond to meeting invitations, but some features may work better if they are also using Outlook.

You can click **Edit the Response before Sending** to add your comments, or choose **Tentative** if you are uncertain, or **Decline** the invitation.

1 The potential attendee receives the invitation as an email

2 Opening the email displays the meeting entry

3 Click **Respond,** then **Accept**, then **Send the Response Now** to accept the invitation to the meeting

4 The status now shows that the meeting has been accepted

5 The originator receives responses from each of the attendees as emails; for example:

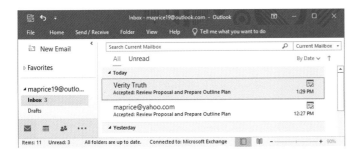

 6 The message shows the attendee's response and status – in this example the invitation has been accepted

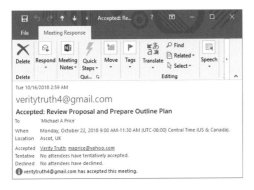

The message shows the current status, so it will show the latest information each time it is opened.

7 The meeting record also displays the updated status – indicating here that one invitation is accepted

Any changes that the originator makes to the meeting details will be sent to the attendees as update messages.

8 As each response is received, the status is updated

173

By default, no holidays or special events are shown in your calendar, but Outlook has a holiday file with information for 116 countries and events for the years 2012–2026.

174

Don't forget

Your own country or region is automatically selected each time you choose the **Add Holidays** option.

Add Holidays

To make sure that your calendar is an accurate reflection of your availability, add details of national holidays and similar events:

 Open Outlook, select **File** and then **Options**

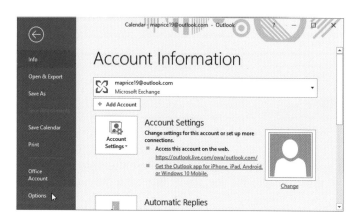

 In Outlook Options, select **Calendar**, then click the **Add Holidays...** button in the Calendar options

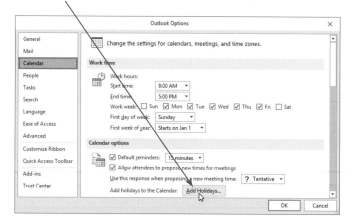

 Select the country or countries that you wish to add (for example, the United Kingdom and the United States) then click **OK**

4 The entries for the selected country or countries are then imported into your calendar

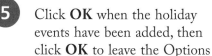

Hot tip

To delete holiday events later, open them in **List** view then right-click a holiday and click **Delete**.

5 Click **OK** when the holiday events have been added, then click **OK** to leave the Options

To see the new entries in the calendar:

1 Open the Calendar, select the **View** tab and then click the **Change View** button

2 Now, select the **List** option

3 The full calendar contents are displayed in **Start** (date) order, though you can re-sort by another heading such as **Subject** (holiday name) or **Location** (country)

Hot tip

If you have more than one country inserted, you can right-click **Location** then choose **Group By This Field**. Use this, for example, to remove the entire events for one country.

SUBJECT	LOCATION	START	END	CATEGORIES	RECUR..
New Year's Day	United Kingdom	Mon 1/1/2018 12:0...	Tue 1/2/2018 12:00 AM	Holiday	
New Year's Day	United States	Mon 1/1/2018 12:0...	Tue 1/2/2018 12:00 AM	Holiday	
New Year's Day (2nd Day) (Scotland)	United Kingdom	Tue 1/2/2018 12:00	Wed 1/3/2018 12:00 AM	Holiday	
Martin Luther King Day	United States	Mon 1/15/2018 12:...	Tue 1/16/2018 12:00 AM	Holiday	
Groundhog Day	United States	Fri 2/2/2018 12:00 A...	Sat 2/3/2018 12:00 AM	Holiday	
Valentine's Day	United States	Wed 2/14/2018 12:...	Thu 2/15/2018 12:00 AM	Holiday	
Presidents' Day	United States	Mon 2/19/2018 12:...	Tue 2/20/2018 12:00 AM	Holiday	
St. Patrick's Day (N. Ireland)	United Kingdom	Sat 3/17/2018 12:00...	Sun 3/18/2018 12:00 AM	Holiday	
St. Patrick's Day	United States	Sat 3/17/2018 12:00...	Sun 3/18/2018 12:00 AM	Holiday	
St. Patrick's Day (N. Ireland) (Observ...	United Kingdom	Mon 3/19/2018 12:...	Tue 3/20/2018 12:00 AM	Holiday	
Good Friday	United Kingdom	Fri 3/30/2018 12:00...	Sat 3/31/2018 12:00 AM	Holiday	
Easter Day	United Kingdom	Sun 4/1/2018 12:00...	Mon 4/2/2018 12:00 AM	Holiday	
Easter Day	United States	Sun 4/1/2018 12:00...	Mon 4/2/2018 12:00 AM	Holiday	
Easter Monday	United Kingdom	Mon 4/2/2018 12:0...	Tue 4/3/2018 12:00 AM	Holiday	
Tax Day	United States	Tue 4/17/2018 12:0...	Wed 4/18/2018 12:00 AM	Holiday	
Administrative Professionals Day	United States	Wed 4/25/2018 12:...	Thu 4/26/2018 12:00 AM	Holiday	
May Day Bank Holiday	United Kingdom	Mon 5/7/2018 12:0...	Tue 5/8/2018 12:00 AM	Holiday	
Mother's Day	United States	Sun 5/13/2018 12:0...	Mon 5/14/2018 12:00 AM	Holiday	
Spring Bank Holiday	United Kingdom	Mon 5/28/2018 12:...	Tue 5/29/2018 12:00 AM	Holiday	
Memorial Day	United States	Mon 5/28/2018 12:...	Tue 5/29/2018 12:00 AM	Holiday	
Father's Day	United States	Sun 6/17/2018 12:0...	Mon 6/18/2018 12:00 AM	Holiday	
Independence Day	United States	Wed 7/4/2018 12:0...	Thu 7/5/2018 12:00 AM	Holiday	

Items: 539   All folders are up to date.   Connected to: Microsoft Exchange

LOCATION
- Arrange By
- Reverse Sort
- Field Chooser
- Remove This Column
- Group By This Field
- Group by Box
- View Settings...

Report Free/Busy Time

Outlook can help you choose the most suitable times to hold meetings, based on reports from the proposed attendees, giving details of their availability.

To set up a procedure for publishing this information, each potential attendee should:

Hot tip

Sharing free/busy information works best on systems that use a Microsoft Exchange email server. For other systems, you may need to import busy information (see page 177).

 1 Open Outlook and select **File**, **Options**, **Calendar**

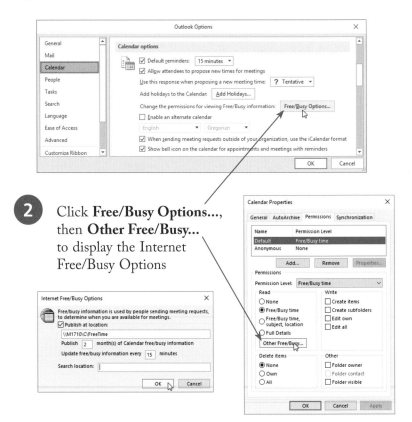

Don't forget

You could also set up calendars and free/busy reports to coordinate the use of resources, such as conference rooms and projector equipment.

2 Click **Free/Busy Options...**, then **Other Free/Busy...** to display the Internet Free/Busy Options

Don't forget

All attendees need to access the Publish at location, therefore this system works best in offices, or home networks if this feature is set up.

 3 Check the box for **Publish at location**, and provide the address for a networked folder or drive that is accessible by all potential attendees, then click **OK**

The free/busy data for the specified period (e.g. 2 months) will be updated regularly (e.g. every 15 minutes). It will be stored at the location defined, in the form of ***username*.vbf** files (using the username from the attendee's email address).

Schedule a Meeting

You can use the reported free/busy information to help set up a meeting. For example, to schedule a new meeting:

1 Create the meeting with initial details (see page 170), then click 🕓 **Scheduling Assistant** to show the free/busy times for the originator and attendees

2 Click **Options** then **AutoPick** and then **Required People**, and then click **Next** to see the next time slot where all are available

3 Click **Send** to add the revised details to your calendar, and to send an invitation (or an update) to all of the attendees of the meeting

You can use the **Scheduling Assistant** to set up a new meeting, or to revise the timing for an existing meeting.

Free/busy reports may not be available on your system or for particular attendees. In such cases, attendees can select **File**, **Save Calendar** to save busy times.

Save Calendar

You can then select **File**, **Open & Export** and then **Import/ Export** to import their saved calendars and add their busy times to your calendar, ready to schedule the meeting.

Import/Export
Import or export files and settings.

Creating Tasks

To create an implicit task:

Outlook can create and manage implicit tasks as follow-ups of other Outlook items. It can also create explicit tasks, which can be assigned to others. To display the Tasks folder, click the ••• button on the Navigation bar and select **Tasks**.

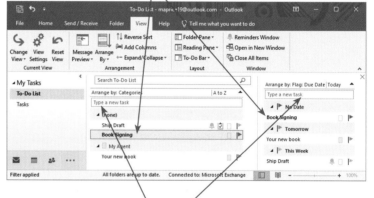

1 Right-click an Outlook item (for example, a message or contact), select **Follow Up** and select a day or choose **No Date**

2 The follow-up item is added to the Tasks folder, and also appears on the **To-Do List**

To create an explicit task:

This provides a quick way to generate a **To-Do List** of actions. Note that an entry changes color to red when its due date has passed.

1 Click **Type a new task** in the box on the Tasks folder, or on the **To-Do List**

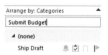

2 Type the subject for the task, and then press **Enter**

3 The task is inserted into the Tasks folder and onto the **To-Do List**, with the default characteristics

The start date and the due date are both set to the current date, and there is no reminder set. However, you can edit the task to reflect the actual requirements.

...cont'd

To make changes to the details for any task:

 1 Double-click the entry on the **To-Do List**, or Tasks folder

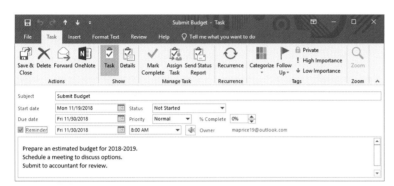

As with the editors for other Outlook items, the Tasks editor uses the Ribbon technology.

2 You can change the start date or the due date, add a description, apply a reminder, update the priority, or indicate how much of the task has been completed

3 When you update **% Complete**, the status changes to **In Progress** or **Completed**, or you can click the Down arrow to choose an alternative

Click the Up and Down arrows on the **% Complete** box to increase or decrease by 25% at a time, or type an exact percentage in the box.

4 Click the **Details** button in the Show group to add information about carrying out the task; for example, the hours worked, mileage involved or billing information

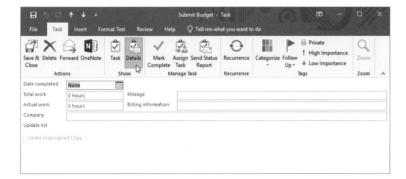

Click **Save & Close** in Task or Details view, to save the changes.

Assigning Tasks

You can define a task that someone else is to perform, assign it to that person and then get status reports and updates on its progress.

To assign an existing task:

Hot tip

To create and assign a new task, select **New Items** and **Task Request** from the menu bar, then enter the subject and other task details, along with the assignee name.

1 Open the task and click the **Assign Task** button, in the Manage Task group

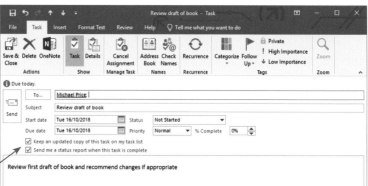

Don't forget

Select or clear the boxes for **Keep an updated copy of this task on my task list** and **Send me a status report when this task is complete**, as desired.

2 In the **To...** box, type the name or email address for the assignee, or click the **To...** button and select an entry from the Contacts list

3 Click **Send**, to initiate the task-assignment request, then click **OK** to confirm the new ownership

4 The message will be sent to the assignee, with a copy stored in the **Sent Items** folder

Accepting Task Requests

1 The task details on the originating system show that it is awaiting a response from the recipient of the task request

Hot tip

If **Decline** is selected, the task request is rejected and ownership will be returned to the originator, who may then choose to assign the task to another person.

2 The task request appears in the recipient's Inbox

3 The recipient opens the message, clicks the **Accept** button, selects **Send the response now**, then clicks **OK** to reply to the originator

Don't forget

The recipient can choose **Edit the response before sending** to add comments or make changes to dates or duration before accepting the task request.

The response is sent to the originator, and a copy of the message is saved in the **Sent** folder.

Confirming the Assignment

1 The response appears in the originator's Inbox, as a message from the recipient of the task request

2 When the message is opened, it shows the task with its change of ownership

The originator is no longer able to make changes to the task details, since ownership has been transferred to the recipient.

3 The task appears in the originator's Tasks folder, grouped under the new owner's name

4 The new owner can change task details, and click **Save & Close** to save them, as the task progresses

5 For each change, the originator is sent an update message, to change the details of the task in the Task folder

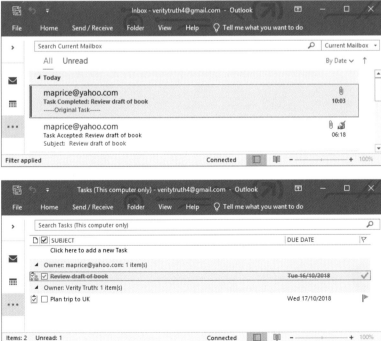

When the recipient makes any changes to the task details, messages are sent to the originator, to update the entry in their task folder.

6 When the task is marked as complete by the new owner, a final update is sent from the owner, and the task is marked as complete in the originator's task list

Click the message box to list all related messages in the Inbox or Sent Items folders.

Outlook Notes

You may need a prompt, but the activity doesn't justify creating a task or an appointment. In such a case, you can use the simple Notes feature that's built into Outlook.

To create a note from wherever you happen to be in Outlook:

1 Press the shortcut key combination **Ctrl** + **Shift** + **N** to start a new note

2 Type the text for your note on the input form that's displayed. The note remains displayed until closed, and it is also added to your Notes folder

> Royal Ascot 2019
> Royal Ascot will take place from Tuesday 18th - Saturday 22nd June in 2019, with Thursday 20th June being Ladies Day. There are more than 8,000 car parking spaces available at Ascot Racecourse.
>
> 16/10/2018 12:07

3 Click the ⋯ button on the Navigation bar and select **Notes** to see the current set of notes stored inside that folder

4 The note remains displayed even if you minimize Outlook

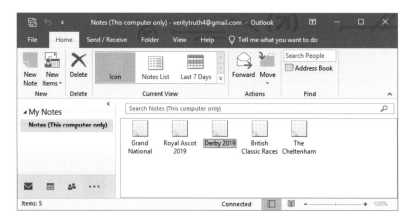

5 The note titles may be truncated, so move the mouse pointer over a note to see its full title – the text up to the first **Enter**, or else the whole text, if there's no **Enter** symbol in the text

Grand National 2019

6 Select the **View** tab and click **List** (or **Small Icons**) to allow more space for the note titles

The notes are of a standard initial size, but you can click and drag an edge or a corner to make a note of any size.

7 Right-click a note to copy or print it, to forward it to another user, or to delete it

To change the view settings of your Notes folder:

1 Select the **View** tab, then click **View Settings** in the Current View group to adjust **Sort** or **Filter** options

The settings for the Icon view are shown. There'll be a different set of options available if you choose the **Notes List** or **Last 7 Days** views.

2 Click **Other Settings...** to adjust the options that manage the icon placement

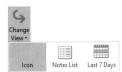

Journal

You can record information about activities related to Outlook items in the Journal – a type of project log book.

1 Click the ••• button on the Navigation bar and select **Folders**, then select **Journal** from the Folders pane – or press **Ctrl** + **8**

Don't forget

You can select from a wide variety of Journal entry types.

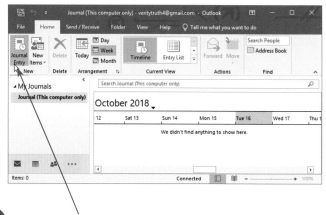

2 Select **Journal Entry** then enter your activity details

3 Click **Save & Close** to see the entry on the Timeline

Hot tip

You can drag & drop items from Mail, Calendar and other Outlook folders to add them to the Journal.

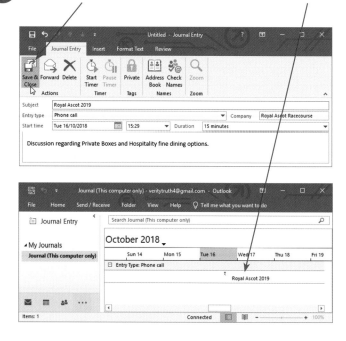

10 Manage Files and Fonts

It is useful to understand how Office stores and manages the files that constitute the documents and the fonts it uses, so that you can choose the appropriate formats when you share documents with other users across the internet.

188   Device Setup

190   Library Location

191   Finding Files

193   Recent Documents

194   Change File Type

195   XML File Formats

196   Save As PDF or XPS

198   Fonts in Office

200   Create and Run ListAllFonts

202   Document Recovery

Device Setup

To examine the setup on your Windows device:

 Click the **File Explorer** icon on the Taskbar

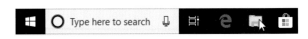

Hot tip

Before looking at where Office stores its files and folders, it is worth checking out the setup on your Windows device. This is best done using File Explorer.

Select **This PC** from the Navigation pane to display the contents of your device

The lower group shows the devices and drives – in this case the disk drive, the CD/DVD drive and a USB stick

The upper group shows folders for the current user

On some systems, the Navigation pane also includes Libraries, with many of the same folder links

Don't forget

To enable display of Libraries in File Explorer, select **View**, click **Navigation pane** and select **Show libraries**.

…cont'd

If your computer is part of a network, you can see what other devices you may have access to. Again, you use File Explorer.

 Select **Network** from the Navigation pane

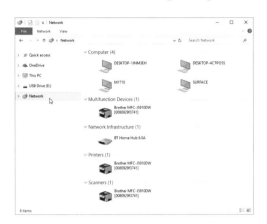

Beware

Your access to networked devices may be limited. Check with your systems administrator for the options available.

2 This will show the computers and other devices, such as printers and scanners, that you may be able to access

3 To check the name for your computer, select **This PC** and the Computer tab, and click **System Properties**

Don't forget

You can also press the **Settings** button, choose the **System** category and click **About**, to display this information.

	System
	Display, sound, notifications, power

This opens Settings at the System category, with **About** selected.

4 Scroll down to the Device specifications, where you'll see the device name for your computer

Library Location

Office makes it simple to reopen a document you have saved previously in a library location, from any Office app:

 From within an app, select **File** then choose **Open** to be presented with a variety of location options

The **Add a Place** option lets you extend the list to include other locations, such as Office SharePoint for collaboration.

2 Now, choose the appropriate location of the document you want to reopen:

● **Recent** – if you have recently worked on the document.

● **OneDrive** – if the document is stored on the Cloud.

● **This PC** – if the document is stored on your computer.

The default location that will open from the **This PC** and **Browse** options is the Documents folder on your computer.

Finding Files

To reopen a document that is not stored in one of the offered top-level locations you can choose the **Browse** option to look for the document, or search for the document by name. The search facilities are one of the strengths of Windows 10, and Office takes full advantage of them. To illustrate this, suppose you've created a document discussing your "Liverpool" trip, and have saved it within a sub-folder of your Documents folder.

To track it down when using Office with Windows 10:

1 Open Word and select **File**, **Open**, then choose the starting location (for example, **Browse**, **Documents**)

2 Click in the Search box, and type the search terms (for example, "Liverpool")

Hot tip

Select Documents, or choose another folder or drive where you expect to find your missing document.

191

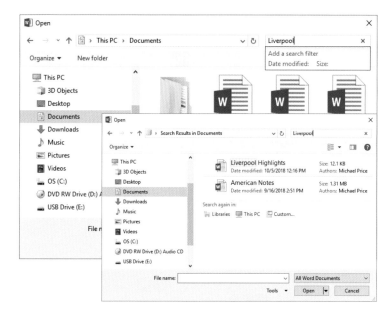

Matching documents from the starting location and its sub-folders are displayed. These could have the search term in the file name, or included within the contents.

3 Right-click a file, and select **Open file location**, to see the folder where it is stored. Double-click the file to open it in Word and view or edit its contents

Beware

Only those documents in the specified folder or its sub-folders will be examined. However, you could select the disk drive entry (e.g. OS (C:)) and search the whole drive.

...cont'd

To locate documents using the built-in search facilities of the operating system:

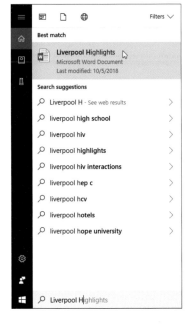

1 Click in the Search box and simply begin typing the search term; e.g. "Liverpool"

2 Matching documents, applications and other files are identified and listed so you can locate or open them

Note that searching starts as soon as you begin typing, and the results are refined the more of the search term you enter.

Hot tip

Click on the search result to open that document in the appropriate Office app. Right-click on the search result and choose **Open file location** to open File Explorer in the folder containing that document.

To locate documents directly in File Explorer:

1 In File Explorer select **This PC**, then simply type the search term to automatically invoke Search across all the storage devices on your computer

Don't forget

Although Word documents are sought in these examples, the same search procedures apply for documents in other Office applications, and also for non-Office applications.

Recent Documents

When you want to return to a document that you worked with previously, you may find it in the list of recently used documents.

1 From within Word, select **File**, **Open** then **Recent** and click an entry in the Recent list to open it

Right-click an item on the Recent list and choose **Remove from list** to remove it. Choose **Clear unpinned Documents**, to remove all the items.

2 You can also right-click the application icon on the Taskbar to display the "Jump list", which shows Recent items. Click the one you want

Right-click on an unwanted entry on any Recent items list, and select **Remove from this list** to remove it.

3 Alternatively, right-click an application on the Start menu to see a list of its Recent items

You can also right-click a tile on the Start menu to see the Recent items list for any Office application; for example, Word, Excel, and PowerPoint.

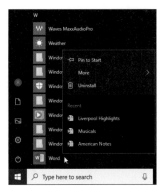

Change File Type

To change the file types listed when you open documents:

1 From Word select the **File** tab, click **Open** and select the file location; e.g. **Documents/Reviews**

2 The usual setting is Word Documents (for latest version of Word). Choose another file type or group of types; e.g. **All Word Documents**

3 You must change folder views in File Explorer to show the document file extensions (see page 22)

XML File Formats

Office uses file formats based on XML, first introduced in Office 2007. They apply to Word, Excel, PowerPoint, and Visio. The XML file types include:

Application	XML file type	Extension
Word	Document	.docx
	Macro-enabled document	.docm
	Template	.dotx
	Macro-enabled template	.dotm
Excel	Workbook	.xlsx
	Macro-enabled workbook	.xlsm
	Template	.xltx
	Macro-enabled template	.xltm
	Non-XML binary workbook	.xlsb
	Macro-enabled add-in	.xlam
PowerPoint	Presentation	.pptx
	Macro-enabled presentation	.pptm
	Template	.potx
	Macro-enabled template	.potm
	Macro-enabled add-in	.ppam
	Show	.ppsx
	Macro-enabled show	.ppsm
Visio	Drawing	.vsdx
	Macro-enabled drawing	.vsdm
	Stencil	.vssx
	Macro-enabled stencil	.vssm
	Template	.vstx
	Macro-enabled template	.vstm

The XML formats are automatically compressed, and can be up to 75% smaller, saving disk space and reducing transmission sizes and times when you send files via email or across the internet.

Files are structured in a modular fashion, which keeps different data components in the file separate from each other. This allows files to be opened, even if a component within the file (for example, a chart or table) is damaged or corrupted (see page 202).

The **.docx**, **.xlsx** and **.pptx** file format extensions are also used for the Strict Open XML formats, which are ISO versions of the XML formats.

This is all handled automatically. You do not have to install any special zip utilities to open and close files in Office.

Save As PDF or XPS

There are times when you'd like to allow other users to view and print your documents, but you'd rather they didn't make changes. These could include résumés, legal documents, newsletters, or any other documents that are meant for review only. Office provides for this situation, with two built-in file formats.

Portable Document Format (PDF)

PDF is a fixed-layout file format that preserves your document formatting when the file is viewed online or printed, and the data in the file cannot be easily changed. The PDF format is also useful for documents that will be published, using commercial printing methods.

XML Paper Specification (XPS)

XPS also preserves document formatting and protects the data content. However, it is not yet widely used. The XPS format ensures that when the file is viewed online or printed, it retains the exact format you intended, and that data in the file cannot be easily changed.

To save an Office document in either format:

1 Open the document in the appropriate application. For example, open a Word document using the Word app

Hot tip

PDF was developed, and is supported by Adobe, which provides a free Reader for viewing and printing PDF files. XPS is a competitive product from Microsoft, which also provides a free XPS viewer.

2 Make any required changes to the document, then select the **File** tab and click **Save As**

Don't forget

All the Office applications include the capability to save documents or reports in the PDF and XPS formats.

3 Select the location to store the new copy. For example, choose **OneDrive** then select its **Documents** folder, and the **Save As** panel will be displayed

4 Click the **Save as type** box, and select PDF or XPS format

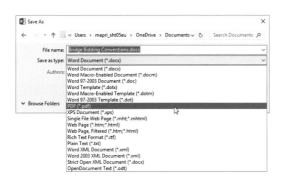

You can also save your documents in a variety of other formats, including ones suitable for use on web pages.

Single File Web Page (*.mht;*.mhtml)
Web Page (*.htm;*.html)
Web Page, Filtered (*.htm;*.html)

5 Select **Optimize for**, **Standard** quality, and check **Open file after publishing**, then click **Save**

You can choose **Minimum size** to publish the document online, for faster download times.

6 The document is saved, then displayed using your system's default application associated with the chosen format

In this case, the PDF document is opened using Microsoft Edge. If you save the document in the XPS format, it will be opened using the XPS Viewer, which can be found in Windows Accessories.

Fonts in Office

There are a number of fonts provided with Office such as Calibri, Comic Sans, Gabriola, Georgia, Impact, and Verdana. You can preview text using these and other Windows fonts:

1 From the **Home** tab, select the text to be previewed and click the Down arrow on the Font box

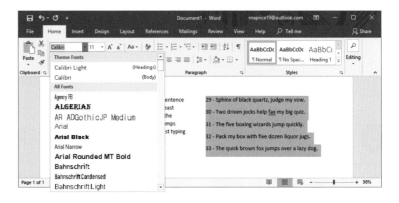

Hot tip

Calibri is the default font for Office now, replacing the Times New Roman font that was the default font in earlier versions of Office.

2 Scroll the list to locate an interesting font, then move the mouse pointer over the font name to see an immediate preview using that font for the selected text

Beware

The font sample box usually extends over the text, hiding much of the preview. It can be dragged up to reveal more of the text, but will then display fewer fonts.

3 Click on the desired font name to put the change into effect

This helps indicate how the text will appear, but it is not really a very convenient way to explore the large number of fonts that are available to Office applications.

With the help of a macro available from Microsoft, you can create a document that provides a sample of every font on your system.

 1 Visit **support.microsoft.com/kb/209205**

There are two macros: **ListFonts** creates a document with samples for each font; **ListAllFonts** provides similar content, but uses a table format.

 2 Scroll to **ListAllFonts**, then select and copy all of the code

Highlight all the lines of code, ready for copying, from the first line:
Sub ListAllFonts()
to the last line:
End Sub

3 Open a new blank document and select the **View** tab, ready to begin working with macros

Create and Run ListAllFonts

Just clicking on the **Macros** button will select and carry out the View Macros action.

1 Click the arrow on the **Macros** button in the Macros group, and select the **View Macros** entry

2 Name the macro "ListAllFonts", choose **Macros in** "Document2", and click **Create**

3 Highlight the skeleton code, ready to replace it

Don't forget

This stores the macro in the current document, ready to run.

4 Press **Ctrl** + **V** to paste the macro code copied from the Microsoft website, then select **File**, and **Close and Return to Microsoft Word**

200

5 Reselect **View Macros**, click the macro name "ListAllFonts", and then click **Run** to execute the macro code

6 A new document is created, displaying all font names and examples in the form of a table

Font Name	Font Example
@AR ADGothicJP Medium	ABCDEFG abcdefg 1234567890
@Malgun Gothic	ABCDEFG abcdefg 1234567890
@Malgun Gothic Semilight	ABCDEFG abcdefg 1234567890
@Microsoft JhengHei	ABCDEFG abcdefg 1234567890
@Microsoft JhengHei Light	ABCDEFG abcdefg 1234567890
@Microsoft JhengHei UI	ABCDEFG abcdefg 1234567890
@Microsoft JhengHei UI Light	ABCDEFG abcdefg 1234567890
@Microsoft YaHei	ABCDEFG abcdefg 1234567890
@Microsoft YaHei Light	ABCDEFG abcdefg 1234567890
@Microsoft YaHei UI	ABCDEFG abcdefg 1234567890
@Microsoft YaHei UI Light	ABCDEFG abcdefg 1234567890

7 Save the new document, to store the table of font names and examples

8 Also, save the first document to keep a copy of the "ListAllFonts" macro – in a macro-enabled document format

Hot tip

You can use your own text for the samples, by changing the quoted phrase in the code line: **Cell(J + 1, 2).Range. InsertAfter "ABCDEFG abcdefg 1234567890"**.

Don't forget

The macro is created in the first document, which can be closed without saving. It is not required to view the font samples in the second document. However, if you do want to save the original document, you must make it a macro-enabled document.

Document Recovery

Sometimes your system may, for one reason or another, close down before you have saved the changes to the document you were working on. The next time you start the application concerned, the Document Recovery feature will recover as much of the work you'd carried out as possible since you last saved it.

1 Open an Office application program (e.g. Word) and click **Show Recovered Files**

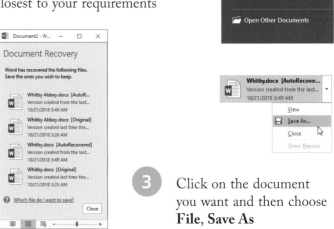

2 Check the versions of the document that are offered, and choose the one closest to your requirements

If a program freezes, you may have to force Sign out, or Shut down without being able to save your document. Or, perhaps another user logs on to your system and then issues Shut down even though you are still signed in.

3 Click on the document you want and then choose **File**, **Save As**

4 Rename the document if desired, and click the **Save** button to complete the recovery

By default, documents are automatically saved every 10 minutes, but you can adjust the timing (see page 30).

5 Repeat this process for any other documents that the system may have recovered

11

Up-to-Date and Secure

Microsoft Update ensures you take full advantage of Office updates. You can get the latest information and guidance, with online help. Office also provides options to enable you to protect your documents, control access to them, and secure your system.

204 Office Updates

206 Apply Updates

207 Change Settings

208 Office Help

209 Explore Help Topics

210 Developer Tab

212 Remove Personal Information

214 Protect Your Documents

216 Restrict Permission

218 Trust Center

Office Updates

When you run your first Office application after installation of your copy of Office, you are told which applications are installed, and advised that this product comes with Office Automatic Updates.

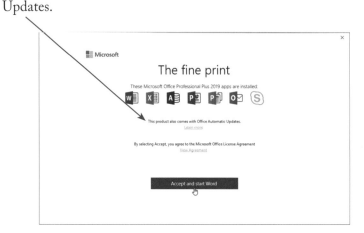

Click **Accept and start Word** (or whichever application you start off with) and your copy of Office is made ready, and the application is loaded

Within the application, select **File, Account** and you'll see that your Office product is activated

You are also advised that Office Updates are automatically downloaded and installed

...cont'd

You can get updates for Windows and other Microsoft applications on your system via the Windows Update feature.

1 Click the **Settings** button to open Windows Settings and select the **Update & Security** category

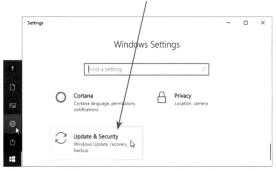

Beware

With previous versions of Microsoft Office, this was the way to get Office Updates. This does not apply to Microsoft 365.

2 Select **Windows Update** from the list on the left, then click the **Advanced options** link

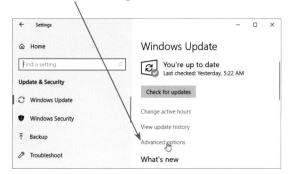

Hot tip

Choose to **View update history** to see what products get updated. These will not include Office, which handles its own updating.

3 Now, click the **On/Off** button to get updates to other Microsoft products when you update Windows

Apply Updates

If you prefer not to enable automatic updates for your Office applications, as described on pages 204-205, you can manually check for and apply updates at any time.

1 Launch any Office application, such as Excel, then click **File**, **Account**, to see your Office **User Information** and **Product Information**

Hot tip

Notice that you can vary the **Office Background** and the **Office Theme** settings from the Account screen. Any changes you make will apply to all your Office applications.

Don't forget

When you choose **Update Now** you may sometimes get a message saying that your Office product is already up-to-date.

Office
You're up to date!
Close

After downloading updates, you may get a warning to close Office applications, before updates are applied.

Office
Save your work before continuing
Continue   Cancel

2 Click the **Office Updates**, **Update Options** button to open a menu offering various settings options

3 Choose the **Update Now** option to apply all available updates immediately

Office
Downloading Office updates...
You can keep using Office while we download in the background.

Office
Applying updates...
Office is updating

Change Settings

To view updates:

1 On the **Office Updates, Update Options** menu, choose the **View Updates** option

2 Discover which new features have been added to your Office apps with recently applied updates

The website may open with news for Microsoft 365 subscribers, but you can choose **For Office 2019 users**.

To disable updates:

1 On the **Office Updates, Update Options** menu, choose **Disable Updates**

2 Confirm the change when prompted, to see the **Office Updates** settings change to "This product will not be updated"

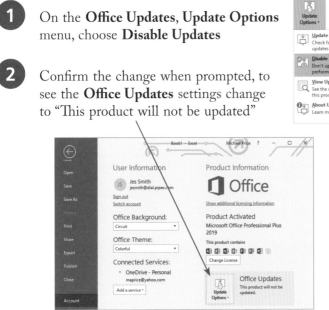

You can only change Update Options if you have Administrator privileges on the system.

Office Help

If you need assistance for any Office application, you can call upon the Office Help feature – simply press **F1** on the keyboard.

 Help opens with links to useful information for getting started with the specific Office application; in this case, Word

2 Scroll down to see the details of a specific task that's related to your current application

3 Scroll on down to see a list of top tasks or featured help topics

 Select a topic to see the specific help that is offered. For example, choose **Use mail merge** to review the guidance that's available

Explore Help Topics

1 You can search for assistance in a Help window by entering keywords for a subject; e.g. "word count"

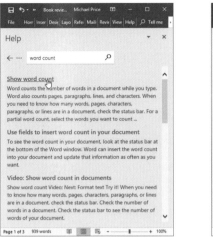

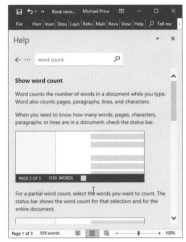

Whichever topic you select, the Search box will still be accessible, so you can locate new topics or click the Home button to return to the initial Help window.

2 Click on any result topic for the details of that finding

To get some suggested actions, use the **Tell me what you want to do** box on the title bar.

1 Click on the **Tell me** box and type the term "word count"

The **Tell Me Assistant** is available in all the Office applications, and provides a quick and focused way to get help with the tasks you need to perform.

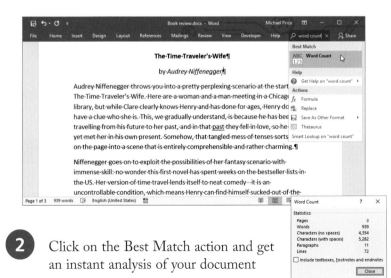

2 Click on the Best Match action and get an instant analysis of your document

Developer Tab

The Developer tab provides access to functions that are useful if you want to create or run macros, develop applications to use with Office programs, or to employ "Add-ins". It is aimed at the advanced user and for this reason, it is normally hidden.

To reveal the Developer tab in a particular Office application:

 Open the application and select the **File** tab, then click the **Options** item to open the Options dialog

 Select **Customize Ribbon**, then check the **Developer** box and click **OK** to close the Options dialog

Don't forget

Enabling the **Developer** tab for one Office application does not enable it in any of the other applications. You must enable (or disable) the **Developer** tab for each application individually.

Hot tip

The selection of groups included in the **Developer** tab vary by application.

3 See that your Options change has been applied, and the **Developer** tab is now added to the title bar

 Click the **Add-ins** button to discover any extra developer features that might be useful to your document, or to add more such features

5 Choose an available Office Add-in, then double-click to incorporate its functionality in the application. For example, choose **Translator** to allow language translation

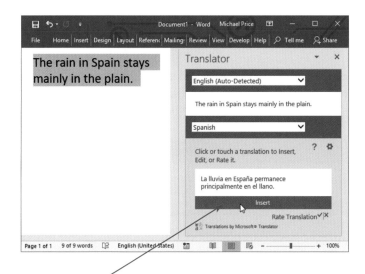

Hot tip

If there are no Add-ins available, you'll be prompted to visit the Office Store, where you'll be presented with a list of those appropriate for your application.

6 See a panel appear for translations. Highlight some text in the document to select it for translation, then choose the target language. For example, choose "Spanish"

7 Click **Insert** to replace the selected text with its translation

Beware

The **Translator** functionality in this example is provided by a free Microsoft Add-in, but some Add-ins in the Store need to be purchased.

Remove Personal Information

An Office document file can contain more information than what appears when you review or print it. You may not want such information included when you publish a document, so Office allows you to hide or remove this information from documents before publication:

Hot tip

The markup includes all the additions, deletions and comments that have been applied. This could give away more information than you'd really like.

1 Select the **Review** tab and **Tracking**, and check that **No Markup** is selected, to show the document as intended

New Book Club

1. We could organize a local book club.
2. We could meet monthly, to give everyone a chance to get the book, and read ahead of the meeting.
3. We will try to find a quiet place to meet, suggestions welcomed. Perhaps in our homes?
4. Does anyone want to volunteer to pick out books, or shall we take it in turns?
5. You can see our ideas for group members.

2 To reveal the changes and comments that are buried within the text, select **Review**, **Tracking**, and choose to show **All Markup**

New Book Club

1. We could organize a local book club.
2. We could meet monthly, to give everyone a chance to get the book, and read ahead of the meeting.
3. We will try to find a quiet place to meet, suggestions welcomed. Perhaps in our homes?
4. Does anyone want to volunteer to pick out books, or shall we take it in turns?
5. You can see our ideas for group members.

Michael Price
Deleted: , or find it in the Library

veritytruth4@gmail.com
A suggestions list would help show our interests.

Jes Smith Tuesday
Deleted: What do you think of the mix

Jes Smith
Deleted: ?

Beware

Do not use the master document itself. It is best to work with a copy of the document, to avoid the possibility of accidently removing too much information.

3 To create a copy to publish, select **File**, **Save As**, enter a new file name then save a copy document

Save As

File name: New Book Club Proposal.docx
Save as type: Word Document (*.docx)
Authors: Michael Price   Tags: Add a tag

4 Select the **File** tab, click **Info** then click the **Check for Issues** button, and select the **Inspect Document** item in the drop-down menu

5 Check the boxes against the document content you want to examine (or leave all items checked) then click the **Inspect** button

You can also check for accessibility issues and compatibility issues, before making your document available.

Hot tip

Select those elements that may contain hidden information that you want to remove. You might allow items such as headers, footers and watermarks, if detected.

6 Click the **Remove All** button for each item in turn, where unwanted or unnecessary data was found

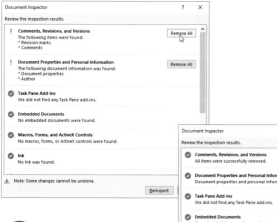

213

7 To finish, click **Close** and save the document, now ready for publication

Don't forget

If you've used a working copy, the information will still be available in the original document, just in case it's needed.

Protect Your Documents

When you send out a document, you might want to discourage or prevent others from making unauthorized changes to the content. At the simplest level, you could tell users that the document is finalized, and should not be changed.

 Open the document, select the **File** tab and click **Info**

 Click **Protect Document**, and select the option to **Mark as Final**

Protect Document

Always Open Read-Only
Prevent accidental changes by asking readers to opt-in to editing.

Encrypt with Password
Password-protect this document

Restrict Editing
Control the types of changes others can make

Restrict Access
Grant people access while removing their ability to edit, copy, or print.

Add a Digital Signature
Ensure the integrity of the document by adding an invisible digital signature

Mark as Final
Let readers know the document is final.

 Click **OK** to confirm and complete the action

Microsoft Word ✕

⚠ This document will be marked as final and then saved.

OK   Cancel

 The effects of marking as final are explained

Microsoft Word ✕

ⓘ This document has been marked as final to indicate that editing is complete and that this is the final version of the document.

When a document is marked as final, the status property is set to 'Final' and typing, editing commands, and proofing marks are turned off. You can recognize that a document is marked as final when the Mark As Final icon displays in the status bar.

☐ Don't show this message again

OK

 This is illustrated when you next open the document. You see "Read-Only" on the title bar, and a warning message

New Book Club Proposal [Read-Only] - Word   Michael Price

File   Home   Insert   Design   Layout   References   Mailings   Review   View   Developer   Help   Q Tell me   Q Share

ⓘ MARKED AS FINAL   An author has marked this document as final to discourage editing.   Edit Anyway   ✕

New Book Club
1. We could organize a local book club.
2. We could meet monthly, to give everyone a chance to get the book, and read ahead of the meeting.
3. We will try to find a quiet place to meet, suggestions welcomed.

Page 1 of 1   74 words   English (United States)   100%

Note that the designation as Final is really only advisory. Recipients of the document can choose **Edit Anyway**, which dismisses the warning message and allows changes.

Hot tip

The Ribbon and all its commands are hidden, and the Info page for the document confirms the new status.

Protect Document
🔒 This document has been marked as final to discourage editing.

Don't forget

Another way to make the document read-only is to publish it using the PDF, or XPS document format (see pages 196-197).

214

...cont'd

Alternatively, you might choose to encrypt the document, to prohibit unauthorized changes.

 From **Info**, **Protect Document**, select **Encrypt with Password**

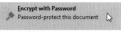

 Provide a password for the document, click **OK**, then re-enter the password to confirm, and click **OK** again

Beware

If you lose the password, the document cannot be recovered, so you should work with a copy, and retain the original document in a secure location.

3 The contents haven't been altered, but when you close the document you will still be prompted to save the changes

4 Now, anyone who opens the document will be required to enter the password and click **OK**

Don't forget

With encryption applied, no one will be able to review or change the document without the correct password, as will be indicated in the document Info page.

If your requirements change and you find you need to remove the encryption from the document:

1 Open the document, then select **Encrypt with Password** again, delete the existing password and click **OK**

You can also click the **Review** tab and then the **Restrict Editing** button to display this pane.

You can allow specified users to edit selected parts of the document.

When you have selected the styles that are allowed, you can choose to remove any existing formatting or styles that would now be disallowed.

Restrict Permission

You can go further and apply specific levels of protection.

1 Working with a copy of your document, select **File**, **Info**, **Protect Document**, and choose **Restrict Editing**

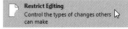

2 The **Restrict Editing** pane appears, with three options

3 Choose the option **Limit formatting to a selection of styles**

4 Click the **Settings...** link, to specify styles in your document

5 Check the styles you wish to allow, then click the **OK** button to close the Formatting Restrictions dialog

6 Choose the option **Allow only this type of editing in the document**, and select the level you will allow

7 Click the button labeled **Yes, Start Enforcing Protection** to apply your chosen restrictions

8 Enter a password twice to protect your restrictions, then click the **OK** button

9 Other users will be able to open the document for reading, but will be required to enter the password to edit the document – as permitted by your restrictions

File, **Info** will now show that certain types of changes are restricted in this document.

If you want to remove the restrictions:

1 Open the document then click the **Stop Protection** button in the **Restrict Editing** pane (see Step 1 on the previous page)

Don't forget

You must save the document to record the change in state that you have applied.

2 Enter the password, then click **OK** to return the document state to become editable without restrictions

Trust Center

The Trust Center contains security and privacy settings for Office applications. To open the Trust Center and display the settings:

 Select **File**, **Options**, and then **Trust Center**

Hot tip

This shows opening the Trust Center from Word. It is similar for other Office applications, though the options offered may vary.

Don't forget

If you make changes to run macros you have created or received from a reliable source, be sure to restore the original Trust Center **Macro Settings** after you close the macro-enabled document.

 Click the **Trust Center Settings** button and choose an option. For example, choose **Macro Settings**, to see options to disable or enable certain macros

Hot tip

Click the links in the Trust Center to display information about Microsoft support, for privacy and security.

Select **Add-ins** to apply control over these. For example, require all **Add-ins to be signed by Trusted Publisher**

12 More Office Apps

This provides an overview of other Office apps that can be included in the Office Suite, or added as stand-alone applications. We also cover the use of Office online and on mobile devices.

220 Microsoft Teams

221 Microsoft Forms

222 Project

224 Visio

226 Microsoft Sway

228 Office Online

230 Office for iOS

232 More Office Mobile

Microsoft Teams

Microsoft Teams is a collaborative workspace within Microsoft 365/Office 365 that acts as a central hub for workplace conversations, collaborative teamwork, video chats and document sharing, aiding worker productivity in a unified suite of tools.

Hot tip

Many of the applications in Microsoft Office are provided by Microsoft itself. Click **Start**, type **Microsoft** and select **Apps**: to see the list

Apps for Microsoft 365 (and for Office 2021) will be shown.

Office applications from Microsoft also include Forms, Project and Visio, as described in the following pages.

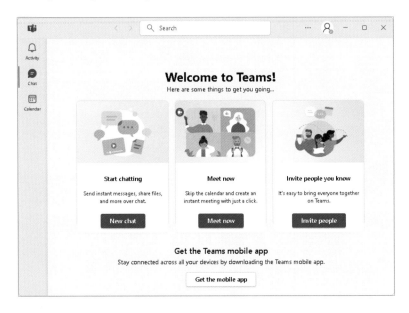

Launched in 2017, use of Teams rocketed with the switch to working from home and it has become the fastest growing business app that Microsoft has produced.

The features of Microsoft Teams include:

- Teams and channels
- Conversations within channels and teams
- Chat function
- Document storage in SharePoint
- Online video calling and screen sharing
- Online meetings
- Audio conferencing
- Full telephony

Online meetings can include anyone, from outside as well as inside the business. The feature also includes a scheduling aid, a note-taking app, file uploading and in-meeting chat messaging.

Note that the **Audio conferencing** and the **Full telephony** features require additional licensing.

Microsoft Forms

To try the Microsoft Forms app for creating surveys and quizzes:

1 Open your browser and go to **forms.office.com**

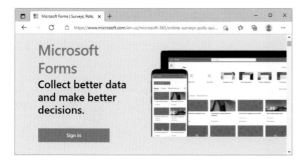

Hot tip

In October 2018 Microsoft made this product available as a Public Preview for consumer users. There's no need to download anything; you do all the work at the website.

2 Click **Sign in** to invoke the online app, entering your Microsoft account user name and password, if prompted

3 Click **New Form** to enter questions and answers and build your sample form using the app.

4 For help and guidance in making your survey, quiz or poll, visit the website **support.office.com/en-us/forms**

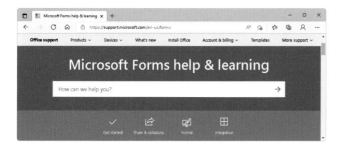

Hot tip

You can use this app to create up to 200 forms for surveys or quizzes, and each can receive up to 1,000 responses. Your respondents do not need to have Office installed on their systems.

Project helps you to plan, manage and cost projects from start to finish, defining phases and tasks and keeping track of start times, durations and resources. There's a wide variety of templates, ranging from wedding plans and house moves to marketing and construction.

Gantt charts were originally developed by Henry Laurence Gantt (1861-1919) and used on major infrastructure projects, such as the Hoover Dam and Interstate Highway Construction projects.

Project

You can explore the features and facilities that Project offers by taking advantage of one of the templates:

1 Select **Project** from the **All Apps** list or the **Start menu** to launch the application

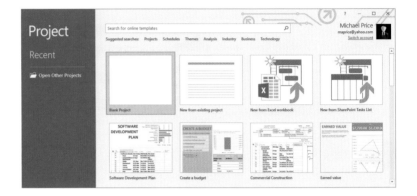

2 Review the templates and select one that looks as though it could be useful; for example, **Simple project plan**

3 Click **Create** to open a project using this template and choose **View**, **Gantt Chart**

4 Select a task to update its status:

  Percentage Complete
  Mark on Track
  Outdent Task
  Indent Task

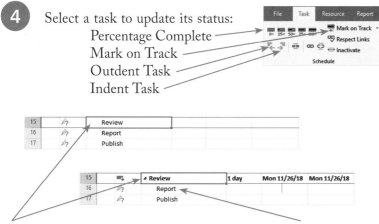

15	⚡?	Review
16	⚡?	Report
17	⚡?	Publish

15	📋	▲ Review	1 day	Mon 11/26/18	Mon 11/26/18
16	⚡?	Report			
17	⚡?	Publish			

Outdent may make the task a summary task, while **Indent** will turn tasks into subtasks of the summary task above them.

You can **Split** a task if you need to work on parts of it separately. You can **Link** selected tasks where one must complete before another can start. Click **Respect Links** to adjust timings to match. You can also **Unlink** tasks or make tasks **Inactive**.

5 Select **Timeline** to see a high-level view of the phases and tasks in the project in the form of a bar

☑ Timeline
☐ Details

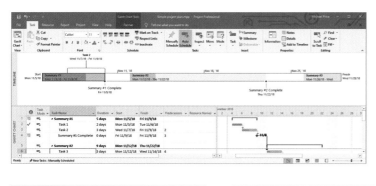

6 Select a task then click **Resource** and then **Assign Resources** to define the requirements for that task

Visio

You can explore the features and facilities that Project offers by taking advantage of one of the templates:

Visio is a vector-drawing application that allows you to create diagrams of many different types, including organization charts, flowcharts, network diagrams and circuit layouts.

1 Select **Visio** from the **Start menu** or the **All Apps** list to launch the application

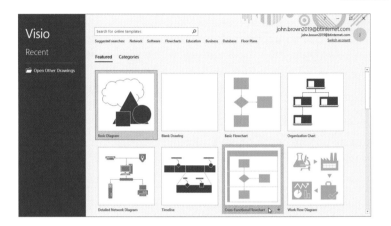

2 Select one of the templates, such as the **Cross-Functional Flowchart**, and click **Create**

3 Choose the orientation (for example, Horizontal) and a drawing opens using the selected template

Click **Quick Shapes** to display the basic flowchart shapes and the cross-functional flowchart shapes. Click **More Shapes** for a host of others.

4 Drag and drop shapes onto the drawing to begin creating your flowchart

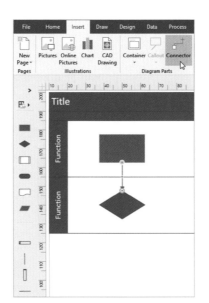

5 Select **Insert, Connector** and click the Start and Finish points to connect shapes

6 You can add text to the shapes and the connectors to develop your flowchart, as in the following example

Select a shape and type its title/description, and select Insert, Text Box to add a horizontal or vertical text box. Click the location on the drawing to type the text.

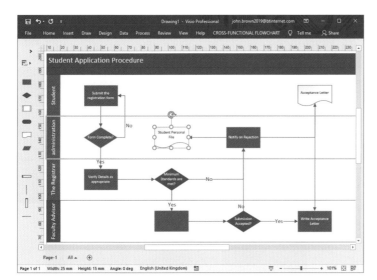

7 Select **File, Export** and click the button to create a PDF or XPS document

8 Select **Change File Type** for other forms of output

Export

Create PDF/XPS Document

Change File Type

Create PDF/XPS

Amongst other options, you can save your drawing as an Image file, (such as .PNG or .JPG) or as an AutoCAD drawing, or as a web page.

Microsoft Sway

Don't forget

Microsoft Sway is used to create web-based storyboard presentations. You must be online to view or edit a Sway presentation, since it is stored on the Microsoft Sway server, not as a portable document file.

If Sway is not installed, you can get it from the Microsoft Store:

 Go to **Microsoft Store**, search for "Sway" then click **Get** and the app will be downloaded and installed on your device

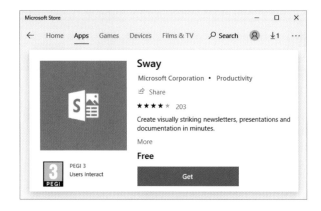

 Select Sway from the **All Apps** list, or from the **Start menu** launch the application

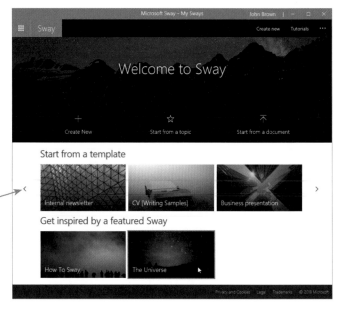

Hot tip

Click the **Right** or **Left** arrows to explore the templates, which cover newsletters, CVs, blogs, announcements, etc.

 Select an existing entry such as The Universe, to see how Sway presentations are displayed, or choose one of the templates to begin creating your own presentation

4 Click **Start from a topic** to have Sway create an outline for you. For example, type "Weaving Loom" and click **Create outline**

Enter a topic and we'll help you get started

Dinosaur, Photosynthesis, Roman history, Higgs boson...

Create outline

Enter a topic and we'll help you get started

Weaving Loom

Create outline

Enter a topic and we'll help you get started

Weaving Loom

Powered by Wikipedia

Did you mean one of these?

| Weaving | Loom | Inkle weaving | Power loom | Jacquard loom |

Create outline   Cancel

Don't forget

To build your own Storyline, you can Create New, Start from a topic, or Start from a document (Word, PowerPoint or PDF).

5 Sway offers some suggested topics. Select the most suitable

6 Click **Play**, then click **Navigate** to view the outline

Don't forget

When you **Play** your Storyline, the buttons at the bottom left allow you to go back or forth, or to view the outline to select specific cards.

View more
by scrolling or swiping, or by using the buttons below.

Office Online

If you have a Microsoft Account and associated OneDrive, you can use the Office Online apps to create or access your Office documents from a browser, and share files and collaborate with other users online. You don't even need a copy of Office on the device that you are using:

To explore the use of Office Online:

1 Open your browser and visit **onedrive.live.com**
If you are signed in to your Microsoft Account (as when you log on to Windows 10) your OneDrive "Files" view appears

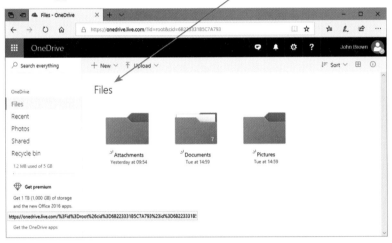

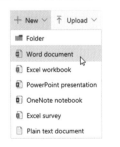

2 Open the Documents folder and select an existing Word document, and you'll see it open within your browser

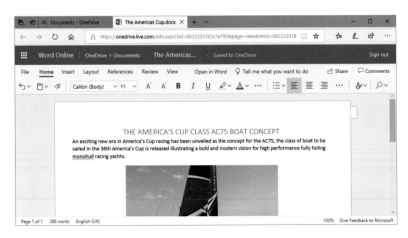

3 Edit the document and use the tabs and ribbon formatting options, much as you would with the full Microsoft Word

4 If you have Microsoft Word on the device you are using, and you require features not available in Word Online, select **Open in Word**

Open in Word

Hot tip

A message appears over the browser and the Word application is loaded.

We're opening this in Microsoft Word…

Resume editing here

THE AMERICA'S CUP CLASS AC75 BOAT CONCEPT
An exciting new era in America's Cup racing has been unveiled as the concept for the AC75, the class of boat to be sailed in the 36th America's Cup is released illustrating a bold and modern vision for high performance fully foiling monohull racing yachts.

5 If you switch back to the browser, you can close the Word Online tab, or choose to resume editing here

All done. You can close the tab now.

We've opened this file in Microsoft Word on your computer.

Resume editing here

Try launching Microsoft Word again

Hot tip

In addition to Word and Excel, there are online versions of PowerPoint and OneNote, as well as Mail and Calendar and a host of other apps.

6 Similarly, you can open a spreadsheet from OneDrive in Excel Online, and select **Open in Excel** if you need the full functionality of the Desktop application

Office for iOS

The Office apps for iPhone and iPad allow you to work on documents originally created using Microsoft 365 or Office 2019 on your PC. You can also create new Office documents on these devices. To find out more about these apps:

 From the iOS device, open **www.microsoft.com**, and search for "Office Mobile app"

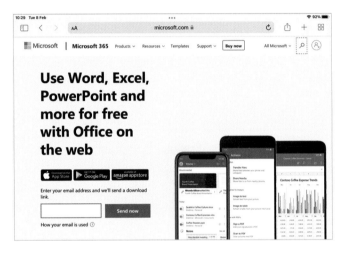

2 The web page lets you download the Office Mobile app, which combines Word, Excel and Powerpoint features

 Scroll down for links to the individual Office apps, and scroll on for six more Mobile apps: Skype, Office Lens, Yammer, Microsoft Teams, and Microsoft Stream.

4 Click **Get the App**, for **Word** as an example, then click **Open** to open the associated entry in the App Store

Open in "App Store"?

Cancel   Open

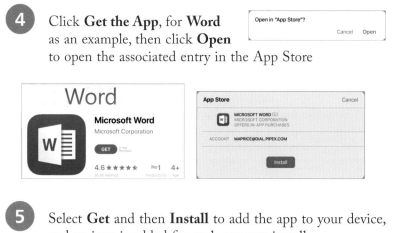

Hot tip

The first time you run an app, you may be asked to provide your Microsoft Account, and the app will be activated and most features will be available. If that account is associated with a Microsoft 365 subscription, you'll also have access to premium features.

5 Select **Get** and then **Install** to add the app to your device, and an icon is added for each app you install

Word   Excel   PowerPoint

231

6 Launch an app and select **New** to create a document

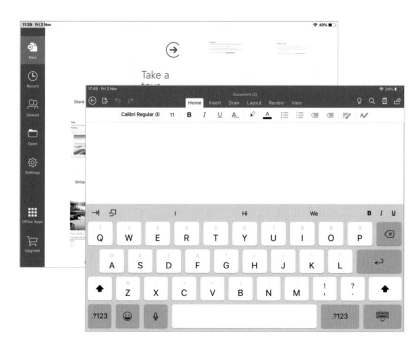

Hot tip

You can save your documents on your iPad or iPhone, or on your OneDrive. You can also edit existing documents in either location.

More Office Mobile

Microsoft has also produced versions of the Office applications for mobile devices based on Windows and on Android systems. Each includes 12 apps like those provided for iOS (see pages 230-231) but specifically tailored to match the characteristics of the particular devices.

● Go to the web page **products.office.com**, and search for "Get Office for Windows 10 Mobile"

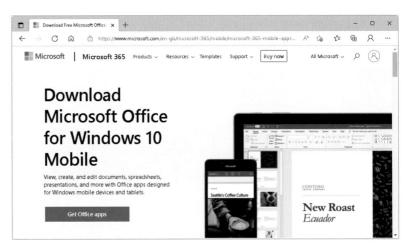

● Go to the web page **products.office.com**, and search for "Get Office for Android"

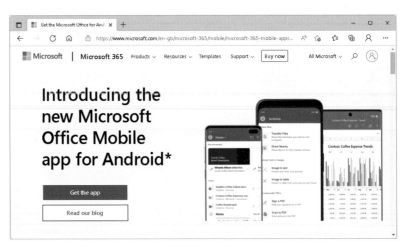

Index

A

Accept task requests	181
Access	
Add records	106
Manage data	104-105
Templates	104
Add caption	53, 111
Add contact	157
Add holidays	174-175
Add records	106
Advance slide	113
Animations	114
Application window	15
Apply styles	33
Apply theme	112-113
Apply Windows updates	206
Assign tasks	180
Auto Fill Options	73
AutoFilter	93
AutoFit	110
Automatic updates	204
AutoRecover	30

B

Backstage	15, 44
Backup	10
Bcc (blind courtesy copy)	160
Booklet	46-47
Page arrangement	47
Preface	58
Structure	48-49
Table of Contents	54-55
Update	59
Table of Figures	56-57
Browser	
Access OneDrive	16-17, 228-229
Bullet items	109
Business Premium edition	8

C

Calculate interest	82-83
Calculator	140
Cc (courtesy copy)	160
CEILING function	79
Center	76
Change appointment	168
Change chart type	94
Change fonts	18
Change proofing settings	32
Chart axes and legend	94-95
Clipboard	29
Color categories	162
Color scales	77
Columns	39, 41-42
Compare databases	129
Compare spreadsheets	132-133
Compatibility Mode	23
Complex document	46
Computed column	100-101
Conditional formatting	77
Configure email account	146-147
Confirm assignment	182-183
Confirm request	151
Connector	225
Contextual spelling errors	27, 32
Contextual tabs	9
Control Panel	22
Convert text to table	42
Convert to the latest version of Office	24
Copy and paste	27
Copy text	28-29
Copy Text from Picture	137
Count unique values	99
Create document	26
Create meeting	170-171
Create message	160
Create presentation	108-109
Create table	41, 97
Create tasks	178-179
Cross-functional flowchart	224
Customize Ribbon	210

D

Database	
Add records	106
Create new	104-105
Templates	104-105
Database Compare	129
Date calculation	140
Default font	198
Define email account	146-147
Delimited file	86-87
Developer tab	210
Devices and drives	188
Device Setup	188-189
Difference	74-75
Disabled links	159
Document	
AutoRecover	30
Blank	26
Booklet	46
Captions	53
Column display	39
Convert text to table	42
Copy text	28-29
Create new	26
Enter text	27
Grammar errors	27
Import text	50-51
Language	46
Margins	38
Object, insert	50
Outline view	34-35
Page layout	38
Paste Special	43
Paste text	29
Picture, insert	36-37, 52
Print	44
Proofing errors	31
Proofing settings	32
Readability statistics	40
Save	30
Select text	28-29
Show levels	35
Spelling errors	27
Styles	33, 60
Table, insert	41
Templates	62-63
WordArt	60-61
Word count	40
Document recovery	202
Document types	21

E

Editions of Office	8
Email	
Add contact	157
Bcc (blind courtesy copy)	160
Cc (courtesy copy)	160
Configure account	146-147
Confirm request	151
Create message	160
Define account	146-147
Disabled links	159
Insert signature	161
Navigation bar	148
Print message	155
Receive message	152-153
Reply to message	156
Request newsletter	150-151
Save all attachments	154
Spam	149, 158-159
Start	146-147
Enter spreadsheet data	70-71
Enter text	27
Enterprise edition	8
Equals (=) symbol	75
Excel	15
Auto Fill Options	73
AutoFilter	93
CEILING function	79
Center	76
Change chart type	94
Chart axes and legend	94-95
Color scales	77
Computed column	100-101
Conditional formatting	77
Create table	97
Delimited file	86-87
Difference	74-75
Enter data	70-71
Equals (=) symbol	75
Expand column	88
Fill	72-73, 75
Filters	91
Find function	80-81
Format cells	76-77
Function Library	80
Goal seeking	82-83
Import data	86-87, 96
Insert row	71
Maximum worksheet	69
Merge cells	76
Min and Max functions	99

Number filters | 92
Quick fill | 72-73
Replicate data | 72-73
Replicate formula | 75
Round up | 78-79
Series | 73
Sort | 89-90
Specific data | 93
Start | 68-69
Sum | 74-75
Table lookup | 102-103
Table totals | 98-99
Templates | 84
Workbook | 69
XML file formats | 195-196
Expand column | 88
Expand slide | 110
Explore Help topics | 209

F

Field codes | 57
File extensions | 22
File tab | 15
Convert | 24
Info | 15, 125, 213-214
New | 26, 62, 120
Open | 23, 26, 86, 191, 193-194
Options | 20, 30, 32, 210, 218
Print | 44, 123, 155
Proofing | 32
Recent | 193
Save | 15, 88, 125, 196-197, 202
Fill | 72-73
Filters | 91
Find function | 80-81
Finding files | 191
Folder views | 21
Fonts | 18, 112, 126, 198-199
Force shutdown | 202
Format cells | 76-77
Format Painter | 33
Function Library | 80

G

Gantt chart | 222
Get Office | 11

Goal seeking | 82
Grammar | 27, 31

H

Help box | 15
Help for Office | 208
Help tab | 208
Hide Ribbon | 19
Home & Business edition | 8
Home & Student edition | 8
Home tab | 18-19, 39, 56, 58
Copy and paste | 43
Filter | 91-92
Fonts | 198-199
Insert | 71, 100
Junk mail | 158-159
New item | 109, 111
Sort | 89-90
Styles | 48, 51
Sum | 74-75

I

Import data | 86-87, 96
Import text | 50-51, 58
Indent | 223
Insert picture | 36-37, 52-53, 111
Insert row | 71
Insert signature | 161
Inspect document | 213
Install Office | 11, 204

J

Journal | 186
Jump list | 160
Junk email | 149, 158-159
Justify | 39, 58

K

Keyboard shortcuts	9, 19, 28-29, 113, 115

L

Landscape	38
Languages	130-131
Launch button	15
Legal Forms and Agreements	138-139
Libraries	188
Line break	49-50
ListAllFonts	200-201
Live preview	18, 37

M

Macros	105, 200
Manage data with Access	104-105
Margins	38, 44, 47
Maximum worksheet	69
Merge cells	76
Message tags	162
Microsoft Forms	221
Microsoft Office app	11
Microsoft Office Tools	128
Microsoft Store Tools	134-135
Microsoft Sway	226-227
Microsoft Teams	220
Microsoft To-Do	134-135
Min and Max functions	99
Mouse pointer	
Copy	28
Drag	72-73
Link	55
Preview	18, 112-113, 198
ScreenTips	9
Select	167
Move text	28-29

N

Navigation pane	188-189
Network	189

New slide	109
New Word document	26
Notepad	141
Notes	
Copy Text from Picture	137
Number filters	92

O

Office 365	8
Office	
Access	104-106
Application window	15
Backstage	44
Common features	8
Convert	24
Developer tab	210
Editions	8
Email	8, 146-164
Excel	8, 15, 21, 86-103
Explore Help topics	209
Help	208
History	8
Home & Business edition	8
Home & Student edition	8, 146
Install	11, 204
Live preview	18, 37
OneNote	8
Outlook	8, 146-164
PowerPoint	15, 21
Professional edition	8, 64, 104
Publisher	21, 64-66
Requirements	10
Start application	12-13
Time Management	166-186
Word	8, 15, 21, 26-44, 46-63
Office Automatic Updates	204
Office document types	21
Office for Android	232
Office for iOS	230-231
Office for Windows 10 Mobile	232
Office Help	208
Office Language Preferences	130-131
Office Lens	136-137
Office Online	228-229
Office tools	128, 138-139
Office Updates	204-205
OneDrive	
Libraries	16-17
Save	15, 20

OneNote
    OneNote 2016 144
    OneNote for Windows 10 142-143
OpenXML 22
Orientation 38, 47
Outdent 223
Outline view 34
Outlook
    Accept task requests 181
    Add contact 157
    Add holidays 174-175
    Assign tasks 180
    Bcc (blind courtesy copy) 160
    Calendar 166
    Cc (courtesy copy) 160
    Change appointment 168
    Color categories 162
    Configure account 146-147
    Confirm assignment 182-183
    Confirm request 151
    Create meeting 170-171
    Create message 160
    Creating tasks 178-179
    Define account 146
    Disabled links 159
    Insert signature 161
    Journal 186
    Junk email 149, 158-159
    Navigation bar 148
    Notes 184-185
    Print message 155
    Progress tasks 183
    Receive message 152-153
    Recurring appointment 169
    Reply to message 156
    Report free/busy time 176-177
    Request newsletter 150-151
    Respond to invitation 172-173
    RSS feeds 163-164
    Save all attachments 154
    Schedule appointment 167
    Schedule meeting 177
    Start 146-147
    Window layout 148
    Yearly events 174
Outlook Calendar 166
Outlook Journal 186
Outlook Notes 184-185

P

Package Presentation for CD 126
Page layout 38-39, 47
Page setup 38-39
Paper size 38, 44, 47, 64
Party invitation 65
Paste Special 43
PDF (Portable Document Format) 196-197, 214
Personal edition 8
Phishing 149, 158-159
Plain text editor 141
Portrait 38
Position picture 37, 52
PowerPoint 15
    Add caption 111
    Advance slide 113
    Animations 114
    Apply theme 112-113
    AutoFit 110
    Bullet item 109
    Create presentation 108-109
    Expand slide 110
    Insert picture 111
    New slide 109
    Package for CD 126
    Presenter view 118-119
    Print slide show 123
    Rehearse timings 124
    Run show 115
    Slide Sorter 124
    Summary 117
    Templates 120-122
    Views 116-117
    XML file format 195-196
Preface 58
Presentation 108
    Animations 114
    Blank presentation 108
    Create new 108-109
    Expand slide 110
    New slide 109
    Package for CD 126
    Picture, insert 111
    PowerPoint 108
    Presenter view 118-119
    Print 123
    Save 125
    Slide Show 115
    Slide Sorter 116
    Templates 120-122
    Theme 112
    Timings 124

Presenter view 118-119
Print document 44
Print greeting card 66
Print message 155
Print slide show 123
Professional editions 8, 64, 104
Progress tasks 183
Project 220, 222-223
Project Server Accounts 128
Proofing errors 27, 31
Proofing language 131
Protect document 214-215
Publisher
   Paper size 64
   Print greeting card 66
   Templates 64-65

Q

Quick Access Toolbar 15, 19-20, 148
   Customize 20
   Save 30, 46, 58
Quick fill 72-73
Quick Print 44

R

Readability statistics 40
Reading pane 149
Receive message 152-153
Recent documents 193
Recurring appointment 169
Redo 20
Rehearse timings 124
Remove personal information 212-213
Rename document 202
Repeat 20
Repeat style 33
Replicate data 72
Replicate formula 75
Reply to message 156
Report free/busy time 176-177
Request newsletter 150-151
Requirements for Office 10
Resize picture 37
Resources 223
Respond to invitation 172-173
Restrict permission 216-217
Ribbon 9, 15

Contextual tabs 9
Customize 210
Hide 19
Keyboard shortcuts 19
Launch button 15
Live preview 18, 37
Round up 78-79
Rows 41
RSS feeds 163-164
Run show 115

S

Save As 24, 30, 88, 202
Save As options 125
Save As PDF or XPS 196-197
Save attachments 154
Save document 30
   Choose format 24, 30, 88
Schedule appointment 167
Schedule meeting 177
Scientific calculator 140
Scroll bar 15, 44, 123
Search
   Files 191-192
   Function Library 80-81
   Help 208-209
   Templates 62-63, 120-122
Selection mode 28
Select text 28-29
Series 73
Settings 189, 205
Shapes 224-225
Sharing options 15
Show levels 35
Show libraries 188
Slide Sorter 124
Sort 89-90
Specific data 93
Spelling 27, 31
Spreadsheet
   Auto Fill Options 73
   AutoFilter 92
   Blank workbook 68
   Charts 94-95
   Columns, insert 71
   Computed column 100-101
   Create new 68
   Enter data 70-71
   Fill handle 72-73
   Filters 91
   Formatting 76-77

Formulas 80
Freeze top row 88
Functions 78-81, 98-99, 102-103
   Find 80-81
Goal seeking 82-83
Hide columns 93
Import data 86-87
Import lists 96
Navigation 69
Pie chart 94
Quick fill 72-73
Rows, insert 71
Scenario Manager 83
Size 69
Sorting 89-90
Sums 74-75
Table 97
   Lookup 102-103
   Total Row 98
  Templates 84
  Text Import Wizard 86
  What-if analysis 83
Spreadsheet Compare 132-133
Start Access 104-105
Start application 12-13
Start Excel 68-69
Start new line 27
Start Outlook 146-147
Start presentation 108-109
Start Publisher 64
Start Word 14
Status bar 15, 27
  Language 46
  Word count 40
Sticky notes 184
Storyboard 226
Storyline 227
Styles 48
Subscribe to newsletter 150-151
Subscribe to RSS feed 163-164
Subtitle 60
Sum 74-75
Summary 117
Sway 226-227
System search 192
System specifications 10

T

Tab bar 15, 19, 148
Table lookup 102-103

Table of Contents 54-55, 59
Table of Figures 56-57
Table totals 98-99
Templates 62-64, 104-105, 120-122
Third-party Office tools 138
Timeline 223
Title 60
To-Do 134-135
Trust Center 218

U

Undo 20
Unformatted text 43
Unsubscribe 158
Update Table of Contents 59

V

Vector drawing 224
View buttons 15
Views 116-117
Visio 220, 224-225

W

Windows 10 tools 140
Windows Settings 205
Windows Update 204-205
  Change settings 207
Word 15
  Add caption 53
  Apply styles 33
  AutoRecover 30
  Booklet 46-47
  Change proofing settings 32
  Clipboard 29
  Columns 39, 41-42
  Complex document 46
  Contextual spelling errors 27, 32
  Convert text to table 42
  Copy and paste 27
  Copy text 28-29
  Count 40
  Create document 26
  Create table 41

Enter text	27
Field codes	57
Format Painter	33
Grammar	27, 31
Import text	50-51, 58
Insert picture	36-37, 52-53
Justify	39, 58
Landscape	38
Line break	49-50
Margins	38, 44, 47
Move text	28-29
New document	26
Orientation	38, 47
Outline view	34-35
Page layout	38-39, 47
Page Setup	38-39
Paper size	38, 44, 47
Paste Special	43
Portrait	38
Position picture	37, 52
Preface	58
Print document	44
Proofing errors	27, 31
Quick Print	44
Readability statistics	40
Repeat style	33
Resize picture	37
Rows	41-42
Save document	30
Selection mode	28
Select text	28-29
Show levels	35
Spelling	27, 31
Start new line	27
Subtitle	60
Table of Contents	54-55, 59
Table of Figures	56-57
Templates	62-63
Title	60
Unformatted text	43
Update Table of Contents	59
WordArt	60-61
XML file format	195-196
WordArt	60-61
Word count	40
Workbook	69
Working with the Ribbon	19

X

XML file format	195-196
XPS (XML Paper Specification)	196-197, 214

Y

Yearly events	174

Z

Zoom button	116, 119
Zoom level	15
Zoom slider	44, 116, 123